THROUGH THE YEAR
with ALAN ECCLESTONE

THROUGH THE YEAR
with ALAN ECCLESTONE

Compiled by Jim Cotter

CAIRNS PUBLICATIONS · SHEFFIELD
in association with
ARTHUR JAMES LTD · BERKHAMSTED
1997

© Estate of Alan Ecclestone 1997

ISBN 0 85305 421 5

Cairns Publications
47 Firth Park Avenue, Sheffield S5 6HF

Arthur James Ltd
70 Cross Oak Road, Berkhamsted, Herts HP4 3HZ

Further copies of this book
and other Cairns Publications
can be obtained from Arthur James Ltd

*Typeset in Monotype Baskerville by
Strathmore Publishing Services, London N7*

*Printed in Great Britain by
Ipswich Book Company, Ipswich, Suffolk*

CONTENTS

PREFACE

ALAN ECCLESTONE wrote four books in his retirement: on prayer, on the Frenchman Charles Péguy, on the relationship between Christians and Jews, and on St John's Gospel. Their titles were *Yes to God*, *A Staircase for Silence*, *The Night Sky of the Lord*, and *The Scaffolding of Spirit*. They were all published by Darton, Longman, and Todd in 1975, 1977, 1980, and 1987 respectively, and all are now out of print. I am grateful to the publisher for permission to use the extracts which go to make up these 'thoughts for the day'.

Alan Ecclestone's mind was a rich store, his thinking was deep, his mode of expression densely packed. It takes a good deal of concentration to work your way through his books, and there are so many flashes of insight that you want to pause and ruminate. Indeed there are so many that it is difficult to persevere to the end. It was only in preparing this volume that I myself read all of *Yes to God* for the first time. I also found that many of his sentences and paragraphs can stand on their own, so finely have they been carved. Each of them provides more than enough for a day's reflection.

I have made no attempt to find passages suited to particular times and seasons. The extracts are simply placed according to the order in which the books were written. My choices have been guided by the suggestions of a number of readers, Graham Dowell, Tim Gorringe, Pamela Mann, and Kennedy Thom. I am grateful to them, as I am for various comments from members of the Ecclestone family.

One reaction was the desire to include every single selection that I initially chose – some five hundred. If you the reader are thirsting for more after you have read this book, I can but suggest you go hunting in second-hand bookshops. Another reaction was to prune so extensively as to leave only sixty or so quintessentially Ecclestone epigrams. That would have made for a very slim volume, perhaps better, perhaps simply different. In the end I decided to go for something between luxuriant tropical foliage and desert cacti.

Alan Ecclestone's voice was that of a prophet. His own definition of the word was autobiographical: one who "searches for the truth in every human situation and tells us what it looks like no matter how unpopular or demanding it is." He was never a comfortable person to listen to, to read, or to live with. The content was craggy, the voice gravelly. He was concerned to keep us loyal to the *requirements* of God, and *Yes to God* is a passionate plea that we should refuse all sentimentality in prayer, that its demands that we should be truthful should connect with the detail of our lives, both personal and political. Charles Péguy was a great exemplar, another uncomfortable figure whose passion was to combine 'mystique' with 'politique' in the France of a hundred years ago. *A Staircase for Silence* may not have led many people to the lengthy, sometimes turgid, poetry of Péguy, but it challenges us to embrace a more exhilarating and demanding spirituality and practice than the usual more homely English variants. Then in *The Night Sky of the Lord* Alan focused on a burning issue of our century: the Holocaust in Poland and Germany, the implications of the Church's mindset towards the Jews over the centuries, and Christianity's distortions in not following the Jews by taking history seriously, and the God who has to do with His people in that history. Lastly, he took seriously the thinking of one contemporary Christian caught up in the maelstrom of the Nazi years in Germany – Dietrich Bonhoeffer. His intimation of a coming 'religionless Christianity' find reflection in *The Scaffolding of Spirit*, an approach to St John's Gospel as a poem about the fulness of life inaugurated by Jesus Christ, rather than a new religion. At the end of that book, as Alan's parting suggestion to us, he encouraged us to read that Gospel as sections of a poem over a three-month period, much as we might use the Psalms.

In his Foreword to Tim Gorringe's biography David McLellan wrote that Alan "had a generously receptive and sparklingly creative mind. He could have made a splendid career in academic life – and was indeed offered eminent positions. But his calling was to the industrial parishes of the North of England where his passion for justice could find its genuine embodiment. Like Simone Weil, of whom he was a great admirer, many said of him that there was no gap between what he thought and what he did. A moment's reflection will show how extremely rare is such a person.

"It was from this fusion of principle and action that Alan Ecclestone's marvellous writings welled up ... The richness of his books is due to their being the distillation of forty years work in, and meditation on, inner-city problems. A theologian of liberation well before the term became popular, Alan's work expresses a combination of prayer and politics which, international in its interest, remains deeply rooted in English culture and spirituality."

So I offer this selection as a means of keeping some of Alan's thinking alive in a new generation. His voice is still provocative, prophetic, and urgent.

JIM COTTER
Sheffield, July 1997

JANUARY

1st January

... every man and woman ... will by striving to be human express [their Yes to God] in unremembered acts or in self-giving with a dedicated life. [The] roots [of this Yes] are in compassion, appreciation, delight, tenderness and love. Its growth is manifest in works of mercy, healing, justice, social welfare, respect for things and creatures of every kind. Its flowering is in art and science, in marriage, parental love and all commitment to delighted patient use of human powers.

2nd January

... we must use the figure of both building and using bridges of communication at a time when human life is threatened by the obliteration or paralysis of humanity's language-device and stored media of literacy. When men put to death the Incarnate Word they prefigured all those mockeries and contemptuous spittings, those thrusts of malice and silencing of lips, by which the spirit is set at naught, the cry is choked, and the bond between human beings is cancelled.

3rd January

... prayer ... is not a rockpool but an ocean. It is entirely right that men and women should venture themselves upon it with ... trust. It is also right that they should learn, as learn they must, that those who pray must be inured to storms and tempered by great strains. "Bid me come to Thee" is fine, but we must needs pass through the waves who are taken at his word and bidden so to do. The waves are not less terrible in being subject to His word.

I

4th January

Engagement without passion is a heartless hoax ... for there is no
real engagement of ourselves with others that is not costly ...
Passion without engagement is a display of fireworks, a waste of
energy, a self-abuse ... It knows and offers no guide to the worth
of what it touches. Its most unlovely forms appear in sexual jeal-
ousy and religious bigotry, its most arid in sentimentality and
wishful thinking.

5th January

Most human beings hitherto born have known but little more
than a struggle to remain alive. In some more favoured times and
places a glimpse of beauty, a shout of joy, an exclamation of wonder, a tenderness of feeling, a thought of wisdom, has broken
through the carapace of custom, braved destruction, nurtured life,
and humanized humankind a little.

6th January

Prayer strives to penetrate what to eyes of un-engagement must be
baffling and repellent, too hard to understand, too cruel to
endure, too meaningless to use, in order to discern the lines of the
emergent work, the future of humanity being shaped, and in
order to engage the one who prays with what is being wrought ...
It is the job of praying to refuse to be disengaged.

7th January

The prior condition of rich, generous praying is an openness of
heart and mind, an absence of defensive rigidity in dealing with
experience, an avoidance of preconceived distinction between the
spiritual life and life subject to and stamped by all the pressures of
the world.

8th January

As we learn to see ourselves as immigrants into a new world, we catch from one another perceptions of the truths that other faiths and spiritualities can bring.

9th January

We cannot afford to neglect the insight and long experience of religious faith much older than our own, nor can we pray with purity of heart until there is purged from us that evil spirit that prompts persecution.

10th January

… simplicity is something to be struggled for, to be worked away at, so that as our praying endeavours to assimilate the bewildering multiplicity of experience of the world, it strives to be as honest, discriminative, brave and sensitive as it can be. Best done in secret and in silence, it nevertheless draws all it can from openness to others and their needs and hopes and futures.

11th January

[In Jesus's prayer] the public-address style, formal, dignified, and a bit remote, has slipped away, and in its place we have, not simply the talking of friend to friend, but something much more, the language of oneness in love. "I know that Thou hearest me always." It was and is the quite staggering assertion of the Christian faith that this is the truth of our life.

12th January

[One reason why human beings go to God] recurs throughout the ages of faith as a protest against a superficial huckstering with God. Not anguish, not doubt, not a simple delight of joy, but hunger for reality takes hold of men and women driven to ponder on the nature of their lives and impels them to use prayer to penetrate below and beyond the appearances of things. They pray because they are perplexed, disillusioned, frightened, because the way of the world and of religion itself has become too sterile to endure …

13th January

Exploration, geographical and spiritual, exposes men and women to new ordeals, and their praying reflects their attempts to meet them. Such souls must face with courage the loss of all the guidelines of familiar features. They must accept the need to let go the things in which they have trusted and face the outlines of a strange benumbing terrifying void.

14th January

We must pray because only so can we learn to live and grow to our true stature in a world (in which new pain has entered) which will for ever disclose more questions than answers, in which our freedom will for ever be the trial of our faith, in which the dimensions of moral and mental pain take on quite new proportions.

15th January

Very many let prayer go altogether. The difficulty lies not in the often complained-of distractions or shortage of time or lack of concern but in the nature of prayer itself.

The questioners ask how praying relates to living, not simply to assure themselves that it can be known to have a 'practical' character, but because they seek some unity of coherence in their lives. They are willing to go apart to pray but they want their praying to grasp all things that this tumultuous world and their no less tumultuous selves confront them with. They want to know how to live with contradictions, and how prayer can deal with fragmented lives.

16th January

Because "I can't take any more," I turn to you, the other person, and to you, the ultimate Other, "You whoever you are," in Walt Whitman's much repeated phrase. "You whom in faith I must seek out, You to whom all flesh must come." I cry out to you to resist the intolerable focusing of all things upon this 'I', seduced into supposing that it could live as 'I myself alone', and finding such existence a nauseating deceit.

17th January

Thomas Merton wanted monastic houses to be such centres of
prayer as would assist men and women, whether Christian or not,
to face together the great problems of the spiritual integration of
humankind, as would enable them to learn from each other what
the various traditions had to offer, and discover what the embrac-
ing of all humankind must mean in terms of the spiritual life.

18th January

There is something offensive and ludicrous in talking about being
quiet and still before God to people who live in homes which night
and day reverberate with the sounds of riveting, machinery, ham-
mering, and passing traffic ... All that we are to pray must be
securely tied to that haunting biblical question, "Where is your
brother? Why have you not brought him?" It is the spiritual homelessness of the vast mass of urbanized humankind that must set
the agenda of our praying today.

19th January

The question that praying asks of us is ever the same: Is the life of
humankind such as honours God who has taken our flesh?

20th January

We have barely begun to take the question of human nurture
where love is most truly expressed as seriously as we have taken
our wars and conquest of power ... Prayer needs to probe the sin
that has thrust aside its intimations of the meaning of love.

21st January

Multitudes of men and women have murmured their own version
of John Clare's terrible line, "I am, and yet what I am, none cares
or knows." It sets before us in the clearest terms the task with
which our praying is concerned. How much do we care and what
does caring mean? It was a theme that Shakespeare mused upon

throughout the sequence of his Histories, and brought to an
impassioned climax in the "too little care" wrung from the lips of
Lear.

22nd January

Our task is to find out what love means in the moment that lies
before us now. We must mine and refine such love as we can from
the tracts of experience we come upon at this time in our lives.
"We have not passed this way heretofore," and we need not be
ashamed to confess that we need new help in setting about it.
Prayer is our cry for such help, made in pain and joy, a cry to the
Other in faith and hope.

23rd January

When people ask for help in the matter of praying they want to
be helped to do for themselves what their bit of passion and joy
craves utterance for. We could speak of it in two ways. One way
describes it by saying that prayer is a means to an end, a means of
dealing with the things life brings to us and of making some sense
of living. The other sees prayer as an end in itself, as if you might
use the word to describe what living amounted to in the end. Our
praying, poor as it is, is what we have managed to make of life so
far. It is also how we are going further.

24th January

It is not the job of spirituality today to turn men and women
into second and third rate mystics, but to help them to pray as
they can, to pray with the gifts they have got, to be truly themselves when they pray. If this means learning to go back quite
humbly to a life prior to words, to learn to be watchful and attentive in a quite new way, then we need the help of those who are
accustomed and able to see with unspoiled eyes, who themselves
have gone on learning to see when most of us stopped really seeing at all.

25th January

We must persist in trying to see, for, to adapt a description of true faith, a vision that is not open to loss of vision is not true vision at all ... we must attempt to follow the always unfinished work of the artist, remembering that Picasso said "it takes a long time to grow young." The note of 'not yet' has always to be kept in mind ... What [artists] see is an annunciation, an intimation of the mystery that dwells in the unseen.

26th January

... the ability to see can be lost or remain inert. The warning that Christ's story gave, "When did we see you hungry or thirsty or naked?" makes clear that such attention is assailed by interests, fears and passions of quite other kind. Words constantly repeated, assumptions left unexamined, partisan choices recklessly made, blur the impressions that innocence would take. All too easily in the matter of praying the stock phrases of devotional and theological usage crowd out the simpler observation that properly should be its starting-place

27th January

There is a silence beyond words towards which all praying moves, but there is also a silence before words, if we can find it, in which we can learn to employ what Wordsworth called 'the observation of affinities', piecing together the sharp fragments of our experience, refusing to be frightened by its discordances and bravely considering its diversity.

28th January

The form of God was put off, the form of a man put on! In the form of a crucified felon He was held up to the world. This, declares the Christian Gospel, is the form by which He is to be known. It is so disconcerting, so horrifying, so challenging to our sense of form, that we must needs ask ourselves again and again whether we really do see it unfiltered by a host of more mollifying impressions.

29th January

When we do see [the] form [of the crucified], even with the most imperfect sight, we wince and exclaim as Peter did when he saw the Lord on his knees beginning to wash the disciples' feet. When we fail to see it we behave as Simon the Pharisee did as he watched the woman who anointed Christ's feet, or as Pilate did when he brought out the flogged prisoner to the crowd. They see no form of beauty that causes them to cry out with delight or sorrow. They revile what they see with contempt. Their eyes gain nothing from the scene to cherish or revere. The form says nothing to them, and that which could, were it perceived, carry human beings through great uncertainty to some epiphany of wonder, remains in darkness.

30th January

With vision, revelation and form, the painter and sculptor are deeply concerned. To see an unfinished statue of Michelangelo is to see form emerging from the stone, to see the beginning of a process through which artists coax the beholder to follow them. They must draw people after them till their feet stand not on the familiar ground of their closed systems of thought, their finished structures for living, their defensive rigidities of taste, but on the ground which is holy where something of the genuine birthright of humanity may be seen in its purity of form.

31st January

The task [of artists is] of opening men and women's eyes to the truth of neglected things; theirs the ability to show by contrast what things have gone dead; theirs the chance to recover a vision of things in the world commensurate with their capacity for wonder. It is the eye of van Gogh perceiving a plain chair, a jug of flowers, a wizened old postman, that makes possible a new vision of glory. It is the imagination of Leonardo da Vinci that faces the fears that broke into mind as he studied the natural world and leads him to conquer the fear "with desire to see whether there were in it any marvellous thing." ... Praying needs that kind of cleansed perception.

FEBRUARY

1st February

To look into a church is still as it was in Dickens' time like "looking down the throat of time" ... The world we know is stocked with marvels; the church we enter is apparently indifferent to them. It becomes itself a quaint museum piece ... The great beauty of so many of the buildings and the dated symbolism may serve only to reinforce a sense of nostalgia, to hem in those endeavouring to pray in a secluded world, while our hearts cry out the while for help to live in a more richly disciplined imaginative way in the world outside.

2nd February

Ruskin knew that looking at pictures and sculpture was not an idle diversion or cultural game but a serious delighted response to a demand to be more engaged with life, to be challenged, exalted, stretched and humbled ... He knew that art was no substitute for prayer but that it was sorely needed to withstand the impoverishment of prayer and to enable men and women to discern more clearly the great issues in life they must face.

3rd February

It was with Picasso's *Les Demoiselles d'Avignon*, painted in 1907, and since then described as "a watershed between the old pictorial world and the new," that the prophetic aspect was most nakedly revealed. Men and women stared, annoyed, affronted, and appalled by what appeared to be a quite brutal determination to deform and disfigure the human form ... It was precisely the degree to which his work went unperceived in relation to vision and form and revelation in the spirituality of the time that made it so terrible a symbol of failure to watch. Within a decade the unfolding of the implications of this painting burst upon an unready world. Disfigurement on a world-scale set in.

4th February

All too quickly the raw wounds can be lost to sight. Treblinka and Auschwitz can be forgotten. The artist must make it clear that our turning away, our readiness to cry, 'We did not know, we do not want to know, we cannot believe that it was so,' avails us nothing in authentic living. Spirituality is not concerned with our defences but with their removal, with presenting us open to God with a broken and contrite heart. We cannot be contrite about the things we don't see as our own.

5th February

When we have forgotten how to see the people before us as anything but material to be used, customers to be satisfied, hands to be employed, or vermin to be destroyed, sculptors must needs go back to a way of seeing that lies very near to the beginning of life. They must press very deeply towards the roots of the human psyche. In a world that is recklessly spendthrift of humanity, they must discover again the sources of feminine courage and endurance, of strength and tenderness so matched, that a new world can be fashioned from its gifts. The spirituality of the sculptor lies in saying in unmistakable terms, "These are the given things of God, these constitute your life." In a world far gone towards wasteful and callous destruction of natural things, we must claim a new sense of obligation.

6th February

[On a man-trap crucifix] ... a simple machine, well-made by a craftsman for the job of entrapping a man like an animal in a snare. We may have forgotten indeed that the Roman cross was just such a machine, much cruder, more lethal than this mantrap here. We may not have begun to think how much more sophisticated skilfully designed machines are used as traps and crosses for our fellow human beings today.

7th February

Perhaps we know the terrible Kafka story *In the Penal Colony*, and realize that the machine there used to write the sentence of death in the living flesh of the condemned, carefully wiping away the blood and suppressing the cries of the victim in a most ingenious manner, was simply our mantrap or our cross made into a little more subtle machine. We are all more subtle today, perhaps more adept at stopping our ears and eyes against the sights and sounds that our still more marvellous machines wring from or confront us today. Artists have at least taken a chance, and we may, because of their work, look further and deeper before and while we pray. Whose Body gets caught, whose Blood spills out when the teeth of our machines snap tightly together?

8th February

Bacon has said that portraiture today is an almost impossible task. How much dare the painter show what he sees? How much does the sitter want to be shown? How far can the love and hatred involved in painting be held together? There are portraits of men and women which do not differ greatly from that strange concoction that stares at us from the pages of Shakespeare's First Folio, uniformed men and women, playing a part, putting on a face, concealing the self, dissembling with both themselves and others. The painter and sitter conspired to a bargain, to suggest to the world that such people were stable and healthy and real. Such cheating Bacon rejects. A search for the truth of human beings takes over; the strains, the misgivings, the fears, the interior twists, are all to be faced and revealed.

9th February

To turn to Bacon's many portraits and studies is to realize that something infinitely revealing has been done with the lips and other features of the face ... we look at the artist's mouth in his own self-portraits, and then again to the *Three Studies for a Crucifixion* (1962) to see the mouth and the parted lips in a welter of bruised flesh. Many have turned away from such a picture dismayed and hurt, but perhaps it was right that they should have done so. What matters for praying is what they do next.

10th February

Men and women once trod out long journeys to visit the holy places to deepen their hold on the things of faith. We can do no less but perhaps will do it in different ways. A holy place is one where some revealing of the love and goodness of God takes place, where we come to see and ponder on that which is shown. We may not find this perhaps as much as our ancestors did in shrines and churches, in tombs of the saints and holy wells, but in schools and places of work, in hospitals, homes and art-galleries too! We shall find the revealing not simply in so-called religious works, but in whatever opens our eyes to perceive with new joy and pain the truth of the life that is ours.

11th February

Paul Klee described himself as living a little nearer to the heart of creation than others managed to do, with the unborn as much as with the dead. It is the artist's function to help us to come a bit nearer, to draw near with faith, to the Creator's heart expressed in His creation. We may or may not be sure that the texture of paint, as Bacon insists, acts directly on our nervous system, but we can take a chance.

12th February

In a recently opened Museum-Home of Marc Chagall's work in Nice, the desire of a lifetime has been fulfilled. His painting, etching, tapestry and glass have been given a home in which to declare the great Biblical message as he divined it to be. The aim of the scheme was to provide the kind of holy place we have mentioned already. In Chagall's own words, it was to be such a place "where men and women can find a certain peace, a certain spirituality, a religiosity, a sense of life," such as the artistry of one man could interpret and make available for others. Chagall thought in such terms, of young and old of every nation seeking in such a house the vision of love embodied in life, the form of the perfect beauty to which our hearts are drawn. A house of prayer for all nations? That will depend on the seeing it helps. His dream, at least, is a gift to humankind

13th February

The great Romantic poets, Blake, Coleridge, Wordsworth, Shelley and Keats, deserve to be seen as heading a resistance movement against the dehumanization of humankind, against the despiritualization which so many of the factors in their contemporary society threatened to bring about. Theirs is a great wave of warning and protest against the ravishment of our bodies and souls, an impassioned contention for and on behalf of human dignity. That they were themselves estranged from the life of the churches to so great an extent is but one sorry aspect of the tragic impoverishment of the spirituality of their time.

14th February

Before ever a Yes to God can be made the creature must come alive to the moment and the circumstances and the implications that have to be faced. What poetry does is to awaken a man or women to the moment, to shape the preparedness from which the response can be made. Spirituality is not simply a widening of the consciousness as some enthusiasts for drug-cultures have suggested, or an increasing of the sensitiveness of human beings, but the employment of all that we have of sensitive awareness and rich consciousness in acts of faithful living. The prayer that we make is the focusing of that effort.

15th February

We read poetry not to stock our minds with the experiences of others but to be better able to distil the truest experience from the events and happenings of our own life. Where the poetry 'gets across', we are enabled to share more deeply in the human response of living ... Clearly it matters much to our spiritual life to be open to such communication, to be helped to distinguish between what is valuable or perverse or foolish. The field of consciousness that is not being stocked with what great poets have said and are saying is likely to be at the mercy of a multitude of such users of words as aim at exciting quite other responses. A narrowed doctrinaire rigid outlook or a delusive corrupting fantasy world may well be the things we are left with, and our chances of sharing more deeply and richly in life and prayer are withheld or checked.

16th February

... revivals tended to be atavistic in thought and Christian enterprise a series of relief expeditions to succour the more obvious victims of industrialized urban life. A spirituality that imaginatively grasped the implications of the age was not forthcoming. There was little to show that churchmen realized what compulsory education, cheap newspapers, greater travelling facilities, new industries and new entertainment would do for the outlook of the mass of the people.

17th February

William Blake was alone yet not alone both because he lived fully in the harsh social world of his day and shared in its pains and its joys, and because he lived equally joyfully and painfully in converse with the spiritual world, with the prophets and saints and the Spirit of God. Few people have been more 'engaged' with God in the whole substance of their daily life, few more transparently aware of the Passion. Jerusalem which was his image of the life of humankind on earth set free to be the consummate glory of the incarnate Spirit was to be worked for through every channel of human endeavour.

18th February

Blake was shaping a new language to express a conception of

human life, of incarnate love, of the triumph of Christ, of body and spirit made one flesh, for which there were no adequate images in the minds of men and women in his time. Such imagery has to be new-made over and over again. Only so can the old imagery be reborn, only so can the Scripture and the spiritual experiences of human beings of other generations become present truth and quickening words.

19th February

Blake found men and women using the Bible in the very way that Christ had deplored, because they had ceased to learn to speak in the Spirit in their own tongues. They were as those who laboriously learned a dead language and made it the tomb of the Spirit. The words they used were a mockery of their efforts, yet no one laughed. The demand Blake makes is so great that our spirituality has not yet caught up with him. His prophetic writings have not passed into and become a living part of our spiritual perception.

20th February

Wordsworth himself was fundamentally concerned with something other, with the spiritual energy that had given birth to rocks and trees and clouds and rivers, in the presence of which the human spirit might recover a purity and generosity which otherwise was eaten away with meanness and triviality. He is essentially a poet of baptism, of the ordinariness of living that the bread and wine of the eucharist are part of, and through which the infinite movements of the eternal spirit are made known. Wordsworth's imagery is always in movement towards silence, always passing through things heard and seen in their most majestic, austere and awe-inspiring forms to a silent awareness of the eternal.

21st February

The Wordsworthian legacy for spirituality is a more detailed Benedicite, the unpacking and rejoicing over and delighting in the infinite variety of things seen in the world of nature, which fills out the perpetual benediction that he himself described as the fruit of his own contemplation. If it lacks much that relates it overtly to Christ, if it is open to the criticism of turning away from 'half of human fate', it is nevertheless nearer to the starting place of the spiritual pilgrimage of great multitudes of men and women today than the Christ of ecclesiastical tradition.

22nd February

Wordsworth also knew something of what was at stake in the crisis of language, realizing that the language of poetry like the language of religion could be falsified, and he dreaded the seductions of both. He knew that men and women skilled in the use of such diction took away the key of knowledge and encouraged a vain chattering about holy things, a state of affairs that many know today when they long to cry out and protest about too facile employment of words and phrases that pertain to God and His Christ. It was the poet's job to struggle for a return to simpler, authentic, honest usage.

23rd February

Browning has an unshakable confidence in the worth of fragments, the broken bits and pieces of lives that got nowhere, the great company of the lost who stand ranged along the hillsides to watch the latest soul blow its defiance to the powers of evil, "a living frame for one more picture". Always his imagery seizes upon the apparent failure, the defeated purpose, the inert stuff, and treats it as precious metal to be refined and used again.

24th February

Browning made it clear that the poorest coarsest human hand was fit subject to be so studied as to reveal the 'crowning grace', and this, not in any easy fashion but as the outcome of deliberate acts of faith ... Always it strives to make clear, whether it deals with people or things or events, that through them "God stooping shows sufficient of His light for us i' th' dark to rise by." The men and women that Browning writes of are, almost without exception, moved and stirred by the Spirit to turn at some moment towards that light. Not of ourselves but of Him is the quickening act, and the faith that responds.

25th February

Browning knew that the eternal Word waited to be embodied in human speech. In such moments all the divine events from the Nativity to the Passion are in our human key re-enacted. The Word may be given no room, maybe misunderstood, treated with contempt, entirely rejected, but it is certain that, because of His love, it will not cease to be uttered. It is in this sense that the language of poetry is the serious speech to which all prayer aspires.

26th February

It is the poet's job to enable words to become bearers of the Word, to permit the Word to take our flesh and dwell among us, to speak the words that hallow all that God has given and human beings have received, to translate them all into a Yes to God.

27th February

A genuine exodus is full of surprises. The kind of engagement in prayer for the life of the world which we contemplate now is bound to be so charged with new versions of old problems and entirely novel difficulties that there may be little to help us in what we have done in the past. We have to learn to go beyond sheer continuity or precedent, to live off the land, to expect to be shown by the Spirit at each stage of the effort what it is that must be attempted now. To "all things original, spare, strange" we have to be ready to give a welcome. It means learning to let go much in which we have hitherto trusted, attached great importance to, and valued rightly at that time. It is no treason to our faith to do so nor is it the easier option.

28th February

Teilhard de Chardin wrote that "there is no present sign anywhere

of a faith that is expanding". He was looking for that kind of
Christian faith that could, with sensitive understanding of what it
was doing, reach forward to embrace the world that lay ahead, a
faith in God "proportionate to the newly discovered immensities
of the Universe whose aspect exceeds the present compass of our
power of worship," a faith that would enable men and women to
take hold of all the elements of their newly made culture and
weave them together to sustain humaner life, and he felt terribly
alone.

MARCH

1st March

It is no bad thing to be reduced to a sense of dependence upon God all over again since the Yes that we most need to make is the Yes to faith. A turning point in life may very well be, as Saul becoming Paul discovered, a time of blindness when you have to be willing to be led and taught all over again to see what you have hitherto resisted, an irksome, humiliating, baffling time that threatens to stretch faith to breaking point and oust hope by despair.

2nd March

Today a new sense of the world is required. The words that describe it are simultaneity, unity, pluralism, communication, personalism, indicative of the discovery of the need for a unified human life of infinite diversity in expression and concerted purpose to explore and extend its conscious direction of life. The Yes of humankind so far has been largely a yes of existence, a laborious painful attempt to permit human life to continue at all. The Yes of the world of today and tomorrow must be that of deciding what kind of humanity lives on the earth, a Yes that not only embraces humankind as a whole but takes note of the interior 'worlds' of each person within it. That we do not live or die alone takes on a reality never before in human history faced. It involves no less acceptance of the legacies of past history in terms of recognition and reparation that bespeak a new sense of human responsibility.

3rd March

Prayer must spell out in detail what [a spirituality for today] means for every participant in it, must bring home to each person indeed that they are participants in it, and that it is in and through such participation that they make their responsive Yes to God. It means an end to any idea of 'private' as distinct from common prayer, or of prayer as severed from living in the world, or of the life of religion as detached from immediate temporal purpose. It must set before men and women the task of freeing themselves to engage with each other as persons, to be masters not slaves of the technological-scientific equipment, to be morally responsible towards the future with imagination and humility.

4th March

Making use of that vision of artists and of imagination such as poets make use of, such prayer must take notice of all that belongs to the social, political and economic life of the world, to the education not only of its children but of all its members, to that personal freedom that gives spiritual space for men and women to grow up in, to that delight and celebration of beauty which says Yes to the glory of God revealed. This is engagement as never before ... We may just as truly call it the coming of age or growing up of humankind.

5th March

There can be no movement of prayer towards the concern for the world we have mentioned which does not begin with the particular albeit common needs of men and women everywhere to be treated as persons and neighbours and friends. The Yes to God of a unified world is shaped in the relationships of each locality, in the willingness to embark upon such conversation or communication which allows the personal life of others to grow.

Community waits upon such communication. If we choose to deny that basic condition, we must repel the Christ who knocks at our doors and the heavens that overtop our barriers. For Christ Himself, having identified His own mission with that of the prophets before Him, made clear the requirements of true worship and of spiritual health. He insisted that they turned upon the kind of relations that obtained between one human being and another. He proposed the quite searching test that men and women should examine whether their brothers and sisters had grounds of complaint against them. He recalled that the God of Israel was desirous of mercy and justice in social relations before all kinds of ritual offerings. The prayer that does not take note of such conditions is falling short of the manner of praying that Jesus commended.

6th March

Much of the superficiality of our praying stems from the lack of sustained and factual examination of the behaviour of people and nations towards each other. To affirm the particularity of history means taking seriously the details of what is done. The Psalmist was right in his contention that his tears and groans were marked, just as Abraham Lincoln was right in insisting that each drop of Negro blood under slavery would have to be atoned for, just as Casement was right in claiming the same for the iniquities done in the Congo. The blood of Abel cannot be hidden from remembrance in quaint stories or forgotten history, for the job of prayer is to bring men and women to the knowledge of truth about themselves.

7th March

Jesus Christ was nowhere more searching in His comment upon false spirituality than in His observation on the facility with which men claimed to be innocent of their fathers' propensity to stone the prophets. It is good that the Church should remember to honour the martyrs, but it is also needful she should remember the victims of her own blind acquiescence in the sins of society and her own cruel lapses of charity.

8th March

What is done or not done to the least of these His brothers and sisters is the measure of the Yes that is being made. Because He has chosen to take our flesh, we cannot set these things aside and offer to approach Him in a manner that we deem more fitting.

Worldliness wins when praying ceases to engage us with the
society in which we live, when we become shockproof to the iniquities and cruelties it admits and too timid or careless to seek for
redress. The business of prayer is to help us to care for the world
as God cares for it.

9th March

It would not hurt the Christian Church to meet in houses and
hired rooms, to stop providing 'services' to meet occasional
demands, to overhaul a hidden life of far greater passion than its
present public custom. "He casting aside his garment came to
Jesus." A new seriousness in prayer would bring such things into
question, recovering from the Bible that note of interrogation that
the Yes of the people of God must be subject to. Christians must
learn to hear that questioning too in what secular witness has to
say about humanity's history, industry, culture and religion. They
must learn to stop asking for a privileged position in society, and
even more, stop bargaining with subtle treacheries to God and
humanity to get it.

10th March

James Baldwin's bitter words to his nephew about remembering
that to be born black was to be born "a worthless human being"
in a world of white supremacy must be heard and never cease to
be heard, just as in a class-structured society the assumptions that
govern relations must be brought into view. The social, economic
and cultural distinctions of society throughout the world are so
weighted with advantages and deprivations that praying itself can
all too easily overlook them. A good deal of spirituality starts a
long way beyond where the mass of humankind has been condemned to live, and 'we who pray' may forget to what extent we
are the assumptions we never question.

11th March

The stranger whose estrangement was his only title to be noticed
was witness to the spiritual task to be performed. The oppressed

may look repulsive, may be violent and brutal, may constitute a threat to the superior culture of the more 'advanced' society, a sub-humanity from which those who were human would protect themselves, but "Who taught the dog the trick they hanged him for?" and whose responsibility is put in question?

12th March

This sharp peculiarity of obligation towards the poor and the rejected gained its universal face in Jesus Christ, in His insistence that the keeping of the Law itself was but a disciplined awaiting of the act of God that alone gave significance and truth to human history. That act He called the coming of God's kingdom. He spoke of it as coming and already come. He charged men and women to be watchful and expectant of it. He taught them in their prayers to look for it. No other word could have made more intimate the engagement of God with human affairs than this, or turned politics – matters of public concern – into controversies between the Lord and His people ... "Thy Kingdom come" was to be a cry of joy, a marvelling exaltation of the human heart that God should make the earth so glorious by His presence in it. It was likewise a warning note of all things put to judgement. Christ spoke of it in parables of growth, of search, of abrupt disclosure, of testing, and of reckoning to be made. The Kingdom signified a life to be laid hold of here and now within the kingdoms of the world, a leaven at work to change the hearts and minds of men and women, a new perspective given to human history, a consummation of God's grand design. In common life on common earth, not in some ideal world of dreams or after-life, the people of God must look for the coming of His Kingdom. It was given to His friends and followers to announce its coming to the world, to work out in detail how to live as subjects of the Kingdom, to prove the freedom of a citizenship that made that of Rome look poor.

13th March

Our self-examination must dig deep. To say Yes, not in the imagery of bygone days but in the politics and social matters of today, throws on to the communities of Christians the twofold task of shaping the inner relationships of their own societies to embody their vision of the Kingdom, and of witnessing in the entire world to the claims and marks of that Kingdom's coming. They must be asking hard searching questions about their own engagement with the world as it is, about the price they are paying for being tolerated or esteemed, about their silences and consents, about their willingness to take trouble to ascertain the truth on any matter, about the style or standard of life they take for granted for some and not for others. They must be celebrating emancipation as a present condition of life by acting freely and bravely in public witness. They must see what the crisis of each decade is and re-order their life to face it. It is no bad test of spiritual awareness to ask in what ways is our mode of discipleship different from what it was ten or five years ago?

14th March

[Of the Church in the past] ... from the Bible could be drawn such teaching, rightly or wrongly, as that men and women were subjects of the princely powers and owed a strict obedience to them. It was a far cry from the common ground of dialogue. Resistance to superior authority was out of the question. What rights human beings had were purely a concession to them by majesty itself. The public weal depended on outright suppression of all opinion contrary to the assumptions of divinely given authority. Prayer for all kings and those set in authority expressed assurance of such an ordering of human life, and scarcely contemplated change ... In the later Middle Ages new notions of citizenship began to gain attention in people's minds. The seedbed of a new conception of society and human rights was being sown ... The churches, catholic and reformed, maintained as firmly as they could the older notions of authority and obedience. Erasmus and his friends, though keenly critical of them, could find no way of altering them. To Luther no such need appealed. The effects of such authoritative systems continued to influence the churches until today.

15th March

... the Yes to life which issued from those who sought release from oppression, illiteracy, squalor, disease, injustice and poverty was made in defiance of the known attitude of the authorities in the churches. Despite the heroic efforts of turbulent priests to champion the oppressed, despite the charity and tenderness that sounded a new note in the teaching on prayer of François de Sales, it was commonly believed by those who suffered most that the Church was 'on the other side'.

16th March

Prayer is paying attention, taking all the trouble in the world to pay attention, to the condition of the other person and other persons without limit. It means, no less, paying attention to the assumptions of our own lives, of our position in society, of the social class we belong to, and whose standards of life we would otherwise scarcely notice. It has been the manifest failure of Christians in the past to take seriously the question of class, to appreciate class-consciousness, to note the consequences of class distinctions, which has gone far to render their spirituality poor and mean. What God affirms, human beings cannot afford to neglect.

17th March

The brief expedition of the French worker-priests, the scattered guerrilla work of communes and lives hidden deep in the cities and shantytowns, the passionate identification of some men and women with the despised and the rejected, point the way forward to a path 'we' must make our own.

18th March

It is time to say final words about this 'we' whose intention is to try to say Yes to God in this world which so heavily engages men and women in conditions that threaten to silence that word. We are first of all required to be watchful, our first prayer – "Lord that

I may receive my sight." If we mean this, we shall see both mar-vellous things of His glory and terrible things of His agony. Do 'we' want to go on with this?

19th March

Secondly, we shall see our calling. It is addressed to everyone, it is personal and therefore for everyone. It is a summons to get up from where we are and go forward seeking a different standard of life. There are no blueprints of what it is like, no schedules of its location. A certain foolishness attaches itself to the undertaking, for it cannot claim to see its objective or destination. It is very open to mockery, and 'we' may be more often than not among those who have lost their way.

20th March

Thirdly, 'we' are those who expect enormously. We expect to be met in quite unforeseeable ways and times by the Christ of faith, to discover Him present "as He will be present", in the terms and manner He chooses to come in. In picturesque terms we may say that He set out to look for us long since, long before it occurred to us to look for Him, but we none the less expect to be found. The end of it all was prefigured in Christ whose Passion was pledge to the world that He would stay in it and be found there and known for Who He is.

21st March

Fourthly, we expect, though we set out alone and are often alone, to be joined by others, by the oddest company that imagination could conceive of ("motley's your only wear"), for this is not a private venture but a common shared undertaking of the people of God.

22nd March

Fifthly, we put ourselves into this with the oddest of all human hopes, of forgetting who we were and discovering who we are, of finding ourselves by a new name and answering to it because we know that it is our own.

23rd March

Here, in our day to day lives, engagement and passion are deeply involved. In common usage passion and passionate mean little else than erotic desire. Engagement announces a projected marriage. With sexuality we face a great hunger, a great drive of human energy, a perception of beauty, an enrichment of human variety, a late biological development, an intense pleasure, that challenges those divided by it to seek and find at another level a unity of being.

24th March

[Sexual desire] is also to be seen as a gift from God, which means it is charged with a character described as holy, an awesome and often explosive thing. Misused it can blast and wither and empty of all significance the human beings foolish enough to mistake it; baulked and perverted it can poison relationships between human beings and between humanity and God. Gifts of such dangerous potentiality can neither be ignored nor handed back.

25th March

Sexuality prompts between human beings those features characteristic of prayer: a noticing, a paying attention, a form of address, a yearning to communicate at ever deeper levels of being, an attempt to reach a certain communion with the other. It holds out suggestion of personal fulfilment, of union achieved, of community known.

26th March

The failure to speak confidently about sexual desire, the exaltation of virginity at the expense of the coupled life, the terrible inadequacy of teaching about both marriage and parenthood, left the great mass of human beings bereft of the help they most truly needed. The greatest features of their lives, for good or ill, were being set aside. The failure was most conspicuous and most revealing in its treatment of the status of women. The ambiguous Pauline legacy, however handled in catholic or in protestant traditions, could do little to help and much to hinder in the shaping of an encouraging sexual ethic and a spirituality that divinized the coupled life.

27th March

There is a great balance of injustice, hatred, blindness and cruel insensitiveness to redress and make reparation for on behalf of women. There is equally great need to rescue men from a fearful legacy of self-hatred and tormented distrust of sexuality which has maimed and so often robbed them of their opportunities to grow through sexual relations to greater maturity of living.

28th March

A Yes to God that springs from a joyful perception of sexual distinction and union, which sees it not as something needing to be sanctified by a sacrament but in itself as sacred and able to nourish a rich growing awareness of the sacred in human life, which can relate its ecstasies to the whole range of conjugal and domestic chores, bringing it down to earth not as a degradation and despoiling of its splendour but as a transforming action, can issue only from a greatly changed assimilation of its character in prayer.

29th March

... the spiritual experience that comes from within marriage, parenthood, marital breakdown, loss of a partner and a great range of sexual problems ... for the majority of people constitute life itself and they want to know how to pray them, or, sincere prayer and play are now so linked together, how to play them out in an affirmative way. How does the "mystical union betwixt Christ and His Church" come to mean anything unless the most intimate union known to men and women is enabled to yield its own truths not as illustrations of something else but as their way to God?

There is something finally unhelpful in shifting attention elsewhere.

30th March

There has been all too little partnership in facing the difficulties of
sexual relations, of inequalities, of exploitation, of open antag-
onism, too great a readiness to put all the emphasis upon stable
marriages and good housekeeping without enquiring too deeply
whether other aspects of the sexual relationship were not
wretchedly abused or ignored. Such a spirituality tended to avoid
the profound questions that tension raised, and failed to make the
part to be played by the woman a clear and vivid example of the
way in which partners to an engagement continually transform
their relations with each other ... Failing in this, it could scarcely
begin to contemplate spirituality playing a more decisive part in
the human Yes to God.

31st March

Passion without engagement ... runs recklessly to waste, but passion engaged with fantasy ... could have no consequence but a
desolation of spirit and a widening of the estrangement between
men and women ... We underestimate the gravity of our predicament as human beings if we suppose that the relationship of the
sexes need not be a profoundly important matter for spirituality
today.

APRIL

1st April

"No grace," says von Hügel abruptly, "without the substrata, the occasion, the material of nature," and if, as anybody knows, the substrata are still fiery and volcanic and eruptive, blasting great rents in the terrain of everyday life, this too must be taken as part of our holding to God. Did we not speak of Him in terms of fire? Must we not run the risk of being scorched? And the sin of sins? Here von Hügel is explicit and brief; not lust but pride and self-sufficiency.

2nd April

Investing His love in the flesh and blood of His creatures, in its sexual drives and erotic delights as in its patient endurance and cherishing of beauty, God took the risk that it would be defiled and maimed, mocked and exploited. He did not reserve this gift of Himself in love till human beings had grown wise or tender-hearted enough to value and use it well. He uttered His Yes in the flesh and waited for our response. Our Yes in sexuality has been long delayed, and even now is pronounced in hesitant fashion.

3rd April

... sexuality, as men and women in moments of truth well know, is not something that they themselves dispose, but carries its own intention, and that not a purely biological one, but something much more inclusive that may fairly be called the creative will of God at work in humankind. Conjugal union represents that creative-redemptive act in our midst. It is most intimately personal and inclusive of all life. It can be reduced to a mere mockery of this as much by selfish self-centred marital egoism as by a profligate squandering of its treasures. In spite of Don Juan affectations down the ages, men have known this throughout; sex has retained a problematic character, a sense of shame has haunted the manifest inability of the conscious will to exercise complete control of a man's mind and body; a yearning for completion in the woman and that beyond-herself which she represents has never ceased to inspire men to attempt in fear and trembling that which bespeaks not conquest nor possession but union itself.

4th April

The Yes to God takes flesh with dreadful suffering but 'it moves', survives the hatred and the fear which would reject it, and carries its note of hope to all successive generations. It is rooted in that which is common to all, in the life of each person whose earliest knowledge of love comes simply from being touched and held and fed by another, whose growth to personhood comes through that baffling and painful distinction from the other, whose hope of true life comes with the experience of being drawn to love the other, to make of it a glad and trustful Yes.

5th April

It is hardly enough to walk through the streets crying "Woe to the bloody city." The word of the Gospel is a summons to humanity at such a time to look up, to expect to see, not easy answers, certainly not the blowing away of spectres, but evidence that God has not forsaken His people. His engagement with them still stands. The business of prayer is still to discern in what ways our response to that engagement is to be made. Prayer seeks to see where the mortice and tenon, the dovetailing of eternal and temporal things, has come awry, and how re-engagement in penitence and hope may be made.

6th April

Human life in its increasingly crowded condition needs organization for a great many aspects of its well-being. The life of a great city is inconceivable without it. But organization can do no more than put people and goods into certain places. It is the servant of certain assumptions about the nature of human beings and their good life. It usurps the place of the divine when it hides from men and women the engagement with God that has pronounced them to be His people and related them to one another as members of one body, when it ignores or denies the transcendent element in each person, and imposes its own categorization upon their lives. What Buber calls 'politicization', the treatment of all human affairs from the angle of reasons of state, follows swiftly upon the ousting of all claims but those of the individual. Individuals can only be organized, and if human beings be no more than this then organization is God.

7th April

Individualism thus comes full circle to a collectivism that cannot afford to tolerate deviation. It is not deterred from dealing with dissenters in inhuman and degrading ways for it is itself the outcome of a depersonalized conception of human nature. The alienation of person from person and the reduction of human beings to economic tools ... become the premise of political action, and for the Yes to God there is substituted a periodic demand for a Yes of approval from the subjects of the organization. Bigger and more vociferous assemblies of the organized become a feature of politicized life. The shout is its public prayer.

8th April

The price of neglect and indifference is Auschwitz. To lose sight of the person, to ignore the claims of personal responsibility, to foster the Eichmann interpretation of public duty, is to enter upon that process of human reductionism in which men shrink human heads for ornaments, take human skin for lampshades and film the agonies of men being slowly strangled for the amusement of the subject population. That humankind has come this far upon the road to the rejection of personhood indicates the nature of the crisis to be faced. What was exposed to view in the concentration camp operations was not the ancient brutality of men or the savage determination to do away with enemies as speedily as possible, but the sophisticated attempt to explore the possibilities of human degradation, to discover how the personal features of human life could be defaced. It was the choice of a No to a meaningful notion of life.

9th April

... for such watchfulness as Christ coupled with prayer is not simply observation of what appears to be going on – the trial of an unknown political prisoner, or the destruction of a people whom nobody has ever heard of – but radical doubt and questioning of what is being taken for granted in the social order that obtains. A Church called Christian, remembering the 'Son of Man' exposed to ridicule, degradation, and death, must always be asking who this is that is thus mocked, imprisoned, deprived, and thrust from sight. Things all too easily go unperceived because human beings simply do not want to see.

10th April

Such spirituality does not blur the distinction between divine and human, but insists that the miracle of personal intercourse lies in the relating of the two, steadily approaching the sense of the personal in order to give adequate expression to its faith. For the Hebrew assertion that "the Lord God is between me and you for ever," and for the Christian the words of Jesus Himself – "as thou, Father, art in me, and I in Thee, that they also may be one in us," come as close as human language can come to indicating the personal relationship. It is understood as intentional activity directed towards the achievement of an ever-deepening communion, a seeking to know the other at the most intimate level of being.

11th April

It is easy to forget that the circumstances in which the attempts to speak of God were made were not speculative exercises but protracted efforts to deal with human experience, to put into words that which men and women had seen and heard, to be honest and truthful about it. Their very inadequacy confesses their recognition of that which must for ever break through language and escape. They were struggling to 'describe' the godhead and the dealings of God with humankind ... The immensity of their task is clear. They came up with the word person, awkwardly conceived then, greatly neglected since, but desperately needed now if the Yes that we are trying to make to God in the world today is to have any life of its own. Person sums up both our human predicament and our hope in God.

12th April

A doctrine which purports to speak of the absolute mystery that is at the heart of all it believes and knows is in great danger of becoming no doctrine at all if it cannot be rooted and grounded and perpetually rediscovered in the everyday life of men and women, in the heartfelt knowledge of those who confess such a faith. If such be the meaning of secularized knowledge, then secularization must be the constant movement of the spirit at work. It must be for ever emptying itself, as He emptied Himself, of such glory as might separate it from that which it loves. The Passion is the putting off of all things that the divine engagement may be entire, a secularization of the eternal that creatures of time might inherit eternal life. Prayer must continually reground itself therefore to speak that which we know from our personal life.

13th April

Judgment does and must ever begin with the house of God. It is here that huckstering can be most truly rapacious, and the hurt that ensues most deadly. If the personal means something less than, and in all too many cases hardly anything of, the mystery of God made manifest in human life, it is to the absence of the experience of true community in the life of the churches and religious bodies that this must be traced. Sin can have no more deadly expression than in putting asunder persons and thus blocking up all the channels through which their lives as people of God should be nurtured.

14th April

Congregations and fellowships are all too often aggregations of people who never get any nearer to speaking a common language growing in a common mind, acting with common purpose and praying in one spirit. Their members are just as exposed to depersonalization as those who remain outside them and make no professions of faith in a unifying Spirit and a Body of Christ. Priority in discipleship must lie in deliberate seeking of ways to assemble such bodies of people to find out together what personal relationships mean. Only so does the great inheritance of Trinitarian faith become for each member of them a truly liberating and energizing force.

15th April

God is said to talk with Abraham as a man talks with his friend, and on this footing God questions, replies, reasons and pleads with human beings in order that they may learn to answer for themselves and do so with an increasing understanding of what they are called upon to do.

16th April

In such a relationship between persons the element of trust permits the answering Yes to be shaped in perfect freedom. Servanthood gives place to friendship, and the Passion involved in such engagement finds its most poignant expression in the face to face encounter of Jesus with Judas in the Garden of Gethsemane with the words "Friend, wherefore art thou come?" The divine initiative seeks to elicit from the loved friend that truth without which the reality of personhood cannot be known, but which also affirms that nothing whatever can break its intentional love.

17th April

This Biblical understanding of human life does not begin as so much of contemporary thinking begins with the separate existence of men and women but with those relationships which envelop them throughout life. It sees them not as restrictions upon the freedom of an individual but as the conditions for the well-being and enhancement of life. It uses the experience of family ties and national membership together with the notions of the body and buildings, however limited and defective these may be, to express the full sense of incorporation, sustaining and related-ness that holds up each life to stand before God.

18th April

We in our learning to say Yes to God are required to approach each other as apprentices to the mystery of personal recognition, to take infinite trouble to grow into it, and to know within our-selves the transfiguring outcome of being sought out and known in this way. The light in which the reality of human life is thus seen is the presence itself, the Shekinah that has approached and filled the area of meeting with its revealing splendour. Before ever words are spoken, and beyond any words that may be uttered, those included in it know that they are loved.

19th April

Human beings are nevertheless slow and fearful in respect of the personal. Not all those who met Jesus Christ met on such ground. His sternest, saddest condemnation was made of men of great apparent religious devotion whose piety was a mask ... Personal relationship was excluded and the great channel of apprehending the truth in life choked with a self-regarding deceit. Surrendered to the business of 'seeming', such men became so fearful of having the mask torn away, that they moved quickly to destroy the person who confronted them.

20th April

We cannot cultivate a private version of personal life, for person-hood is a recognition of total indebtedness on the one hand and total requiredness on the other. Prayer must keep before us that polarity since individualized worldliness hates to acknowledge indebtedness and affects to despise requiredness.

21st April

To live and to pray in a personal way must mean a lifelong struggle against whatever expresses contempt or hatred or indifference to men and women of any kind. It means identification with the despised, not because they are better people than those who ill-treat them or are welcoming to those who endeavour to help them, but simply because they are needed and needy. A humanity that is broken up into various 'worlds', superpowers and backward peoples, immigrants, refugees, displaced persons, ruling and servant classes, is a world shouting No to God ...

22nd April

... to speak of the pentecostal experience is not to talk of something outside the mainstream of human awareness today or of a peculiar form of spirituality, but to acknowledge what is most living in the response of humankind. Although we are but at the beginning of understanding what the encounter of dialogue means, recognition of the necessity laid upon Christians to speak openly and personally with the world, with other faiths, with other disciplines, of the need to learn what can only be communicated in silence, of the task of going out to the estranged, has brought humankind to a new attentiveness to the concordant discord through which a new Yes to God may be spoken. The personal is known in the increasing recognition, freed from fear of interdependence, knitting together the whole company of humankind.

23rd April

Franz Rosenzweig described [the experience of] his decision to remain a Jew. He had found himself for some years poised upon the brink of a choice between Judaism and Christianity. There came a day when, in his own words, he too descended into the vaults of his own being to face the supreme problem of his spiritual life. He came back to the light of common day, not simply with the decision made, but with a new sense of the commonness of the day, a new awareness of the nature of his engagement with the world of men and women, of the world to be redeemed into personality, of his own relationship with the students and waiters and barbers' apprentices as persons-in-the-making like himself. New depths in the divine had been disclosed in this new perception of the world at work. The interior life was no private world detached from or more real than the world of circumstance and history but entry into that dimension where the personal engagement of God with His worlds and creatures might be known.

24th April

The personal then is that focus of all the inter-relatedness that gives to each of us our particular place in God's world. When to strive to know ourselves, we are seeking to know not a speck of dust nor the human species but the Word that was spoken and took our flesh, the Yes that permitted us to be. We are seeking to know it because we are sought-out, because we are named as persons are named, because to be persons at all is to find in our hearts the Yes that strives to reply. We are that Yes, not of ourselves alone, but in Him and through Him in eternity.

25th April

[Being "better than the world" – James Baldwin's phrase –] at the present time starts from experiencing the pain of being in the world as a personal thing, particularizing it in the details of what it means to be this man or that woman, seeing such things as parts of the Passion, taking the engagement that is offered in them in an unembittered spirit, pursuing in all things the coming to be of a world which in all its enterprises honours the Incarnate Lord.

26th April

... the ancient litanies whose observations were like stones in a desert, each so like the other yet just a little different, each establishing to the patient eye a difference to be underlined, insisted upon, repeated seemingly, emphasized for its difference and made the measure of the attention of continuing prayer. This is not 'vain repetition' but continual new effort, geared to an awareness

of the length of the journey. It is not the only way of praying but
it is the one which most of us have need to learn just because great
tracts of life are only going to be lived through at such a pace.

27th April

The point is that we have to find for ourselves the rhythmical pace
at which we can keep going in our prayers; each of us has to learn
to change step on occasion and alter the pace when the time for
some change comes round. Do it too often and you begin to stum-
ble and falter. Fail to change step when needed and you run out of
breath and stop. Much of praying consists in saying old words in
a way that makes them new, in refusing to let them go dead by
treating them as if they were not able to be new words. This is not
a mechanical view of praying but in truth its opposite, taking note
of our make-up, age, condition of body and mind, and all the circumstances in which we live. People in bodily pain, in tension of
mind, in old age, in uprooted conditions, have all to be helped to
be changing their step. We have to find the pace that is truly our
own, and not regret that we cannot skip along as once we could.
It may be a much slower pace than we'd care to admit to, one that
seems to make no headway at all, one that possesses few virtues
but the chief merit of keeping on.

28th April

We must find for ourselves the words to go with the pace, both old
and new ones. The words we take with us now, the words that
imagination fits to the journey itself, don't have to be defended. If
they have to be bitten through as our ancestors bit coins to try
their metal, then it's up to us to bite hard and spit out the words
that won't stand the test. We are not to be hypnotized by words
either, however sublime they sound or sacred their ancestry, and
least of all by the specialized talk of experts in their own various
fields of knowledge. In prayer as in good writing the style's the
man, and we must by much labour find our own, drawing upon
the common language of the people of God, our mother tongue,
and shaping our own authentic Yes with it in virtue of what we
have seen and heard.

29th April

… though it is true that the engagement began before we got here, before ever the worlds were made, and will continue after they have ceased to be, it is this world that for the present defines our job. That job is to be good human beings, to find out what that means for ourselves and others, not to treat the world as a back-cloth to a solo performance nor to try to forget it whenever we try to pray … We are to pray, no matter how hidden the inmost room from which it is made, as those who are, up to their full capacity, to grow in wonder and delight at the vast context of God's action. We are to pray, no matter how still our bodies, as those who are sustained by the great tidal wave of His oncoming Kingdom. We are to pray, no matter how silent our lips, as those who join in the dawn-chorus of a new creation.

30th April

Offices, spiritual exercises, methods of mental prayer, litanies, all have their place, and their function is to bring us into touch with the activity of the Spirit of God, the initiator of the cosmic pur-pose, the fiery energy of its unfolding, but we must not be tied to any of them. The whole point of prayer being personal and our-selves being persons is that while we owe everything we have to others and should be joyfully conscious of this, what we do with it must be ours by intention and not a copying of anyone else. To be personal is to be adding something to the diversity and the unity of the creation. It must likewise welcome, expect, make possible and cherish what others do and are.

MAY

1st May

What divides us springs from style of life, education, tradition, wealth, sheer ignorance, as well as from different religious and philosophical backgrounds. The kind of help that we may try to give each other must take notice of this and not pretend that the divisions do not go very deep. Behind us lie centuries of persecution, and Christians all too easily forget that this hideous thing practised in the name of Christ has left its own evil legacy of bitterness and distrust that affects the spiritual health of the world today. Péguy was right in seeing the Dreyfus affair as an instance of mildew and rottenness overtaking a nation. We need as much insight today to make clear that we do not escape such contamination merely by being ignorant of its sources. The prayer that affects to leave the world behind because it lacks the charity to face it is already so diseased, and its death a necessary condition of rebirth to a livelier faith.

2nd May

The Church has tended for too long to treat its members as if they were eternally infants, and the gaps between its learned and erudite scholars, its clergy and its rank and file members are a weakness and an embarrassment to any corporate action, and an impoverishing factor in its spirituality. So much prayer dwindles and dies because it has no solid foundation in reflection and shared understanding. This is to a great extent no more than another aspect of contemporary life in which almost all things conspire to push human life to a superficial level.

3rd May

If communication in the basic community of life dwindles to meagre proportions, if the communication within the parish churches gets absorbed in matters of finance, if communication within religious communities gets pushed a long way down the list of matters to be attended to, what chance is there that the common personal prayer of the people involved will grow rich by virtue of that which every member supplies. It is not the gross scandals that go far to corrupt the spiritual life of the churches so much as the low standards of corporate concern for the informing of the members about their real calling and common involvement.

4th May

What we all need is a Book of Common Prayer, a Missal, a service book, with more blank pages than printed ones, an interleaved book in which we may write the things that are of personal weight and concern, in which we paste pictures or poems or fragments of letters, in which we note down the questions we find we must face. It is the word-book of our life, our attempt to relate those tremendous things of the Liturgy or the Psalms to the jobs and the problems and delights of our personal living.

5th May

Without the constant search for reality, begun in the first place by sustained effort to perceive the extent of our indebtedness to others and our completely recipient condition, spirituality tends to be overtaken by the search for certainties and authoritative safe-guards on the one hand and by fantasy-making on the other. Both of these destroy the faith that praying is concerned to nurture, for with certainties we grow arrogant and with fantasies self-indulgent. People get lost in fantasy or crave for authoritative direction because they have not learned to note with gratitude the singular details of such goodness that comes their way.

6th May

Among all the great Biblical questions addressed to human beings which initiate a new level of dialogue and prepare the way for a Yes of greater content few penetrate more deeply to the personal level than that which follows the washing of the disciples' feet, "Know ye what I have done to you?" It could be said that all prayer is occupied with answering that question. The attempted Yes must needs embrace all humankind and all that faith in God holds on to.

7th May

We shall not think of ourselves as called upon to say Yes to God unless we first hear the questions ... It is an interrogative God with whom we have to do, and there can be no better exercise in the preparation for prayer than working through the Gospels to note every question that Jesus Christ is described as asking, and furthermore, seeing them as the culmination of a questioning which the writers of Genesis indicate as beginning in the garden and which continue to be put to men and women throughout the Old Testament record. Having learned to pay attention to those questions we shall be better able to ask the right questions ourselves. Our Yes to God goes astray all too often because either we grow inert and ask no questions at all, which is a poor reply to God who made us in His image, or we ask foolish inept questions which show that we haven't listened to His. To be good witnesses we have got to learn to get the questions right; otherwise we shall substitute our own version and be content with that.

8th May

The second feature can be described as compiling our own Benedicite, with the help of all those referred to earlier as openers of human eyes and ears. We have now a long enough record of art and literature to see – as the Bible itself makes plain – that no statement, no style, no interpretation, is ever complete and finished. Alert preparation for prayer is therefore alive to the fact that our Yes to God stands in just such need of being restated.

It is this, for example, that makes the *Centuries of Meditations* of Traherne a pointer to what we ourselves can do. We are not to do it his way but find our own. We have our own book to fill; we can follow his words, "I have a mind to fill this with profitable wonders," and we can start at once for this is the day we were given to do it in. We are in a world which is being remade every moment, we ourselves are such creatures of change, and true knowledge of this is the recognition of it that we are putting into prayer.

9th May

The third feature may be related to the Benedictus, to the fact that God has visited His people. This has got to be noticed all over again in the peculiarities of history and the social scene in which we are now placed. The action of the Spirit doesn't make men and women puppets but responsible agents in the creative purpose of God. Preparation for prayer means scrutiny of this world scene in order that the response we make may be discerning as was that of Simeon and Anna when the moment of the presentation in the Temple came. The job of prayer is to turn the events into experience. It means that we have to be asking how what we encounter in the immediate circumstances in which we live and work, as well as in the world scene in which our life is to be lived out, can be turned into the material of dialogue with God. Our lives may be, as the world judges these things, singularly uneventful, as plain and drab as it is possible to have, yet every moment is capable of being charged with perception of the Passion and the kind of engagement that at this moment is offered to us. But the Yes of such moments will never be made apart from the persistent plodding determination to use every scrap of its uneventfulness.

10th May

If praying is to be honest and unpretentious and not adding to the element of fantasy in life, it will be as much concerned with the shallows of living as with the depths. It is in the devouring shallows of trivial aimless insensitive living that most of us in any case get wrecked. Most of us can look back upon a great deal of wasted time and it is likely that increased leisure will intensify this problem, though 'laying waste our powers' is no new feature of human life. Looking forward alone does not of itself supply a remedy though it may offer its own variety of deceptive promise. It is the sense that so many clues have proved to be false, so many paths ended in getting nowhere, so many hopes exhausted, that breaks men and women who cannot be insensible to the shabbiness of their lives but find no enlivening alternative. Such people do not find the language of traditional devotion very helpful. It appears all too often to start from a point that they themselves are removed from, it presupposes a purity and an integrity that they are all too conscious of not possessing. To speak of the vision of God is often to add to the discouragement of those whose vision of life and of themselves is already clouded and murky. "What should such fellows as I do crawling between heaven and earth?"

11th May

We need to take very literally the point that we don't know how to pray as we ought, but not to be put off by that. This is the real test. It cuts our attempted Yes to God down to the size that we don't much like but it doesn't pretend that No would do as well. A great deal of prayer in the depths found no better thing to do but to wait in silence, a silence that was not just a lack of words but a tacit assertion that God must speak first and that we must wait for that. How long must we wait? There again the record suggests that our time can give us no answer in hours or years but it can make known the presence of something we dare to call eternal in it.

12th May

The end is not yet. Prayer is, however feeble and immature, a gesture of faith, the gesture we go on making in order that the Yes of humankind may be uttered and known. Much of it must be like the irrelevant if well-meaning talking of Peter on the mount of transfiguration, much of it will be overtaken as were Peter's subsequent assertion of steadfastness, by shabby and pitiful treachery, much of it will be and needs to be shaken out of its cherished illusions. But the faith that issues in prayer is, despite all these very real and grievous faults, a faith that perceives the glory of God and knows that the Yes He has spoken, the Yes that is Christ, is the truth to which it answers Amen.

13th May

The medium (ie the medieval monasteries) even if it had been served by the most dedicated men and women, was no longer able to confront society with a spirituality commensurate with the problems of human life in the new situation. "The bare ruined choirs" remind us not only of the rapacity of those who fell upon the monastic world to despoil its wealth, but also of a failure on the part of what had once been the great stimulating spiritual factor in European life to meet new demands.

14th May

Péguy's conception of himself was that of a man posted to the frontier. His true greatness lay in seeing where that frontier was, seeing how it ran through the heart of Europe and from there through every continent of the world, but running also through our sense of history, of religion, of political purpose and the creativity of human culture ... Péguy packed and repacked his bag many times in order to stay where the frontier ran.

15th May

Péguy was a man uniquely able to provide what George Steiner has called "a field of prepared echoes", echoes that sound back as far as Eve herself, linger around Orléans and Chartres, and come to us compounded from the spiritual experience of the past without deadening our attention to the sounds we must hear today. To hear what he really says we have to be silent and ready to be sensitized beyond the ordinary range of our current speech. This again is one of the tasks of prayer, of the making of our ladder of silence.

16th May

Becoming absorbed in the one-dimensional current of instant speech we are in danger of losing both will and ability to attend to echoes. Still less are we ready to wait on what lies beyond them. The suggestion that we need to do so is likely to be received with incredulity or incomprehension by many people today. Does it really matter? Are we any the better off if we have ears to hear "the notes that are/The ghostly language of the ancient earth"? More important still, what happens to the children of a mother-tongue when no one knows how to listen? What happens to the Word when it is arrested and regimented to the sloganizing of Church and State? How free are men and women when their words are slaves? Each year we extend our uses of the media of communication, each year the Babel of tongues grows more stridently oppressive. Our problem is not that the trumpet now gives an uncertain sound, but that too many trumpets proclaim their certainties, too many loudspeakers claim attention and submission. Our modern Sower does not sow words that need sunlight and soil, rain and time, in which to strike root and grow, but sows pre-packaged replies. Péguy in this respect is claiming attention that leaves human beings free. Listening means liberation.

17th May

I believe that our European church life, whether in Catholic or Protestant, Anglican or Orthodox, forms, has so diminished that breadth of attentive concern for the world for which Christ died, so narrowed the vision of many devout and earnest people, so faltered in its critique of the powers of the world and indeed of its own life, that neither its words nor its witness stir men and women's lives to the depths. Too jealous of its privileged position, too fearful for its survival, too unimaginative to be bold, it has acquiesced to an almost self-stultifying extent in the fragmentation of human life. The wholeness of life, the life of the whole person, has been talked of but rarely envisaged as its proper concern.

18th May

The theoretical analyses of class conflict might or might not be true, but the facts of human experience were not in dispute. The possession of wealth and power did result in oppression and indifference and hardness of heart on the part of the rich; the lack of food, rest, shelter and freedom on the part of the poor did deprive them of opportunity to grow up to full human stature. The voices of Nathan, Amos, Isaiah and Micah, the voice of Jesus Himself, said plainly enough what this meant in terms of sin. It was eternal salvation that was at stake, and it was the ideological covering up of sin together with the acquiescence of Church and State in such things that moved Péguy to cry out.

19th May

We need a freedom to move at our own pace – as wise teachers have always known. Other people's words of counsel have to root themselves in our lives, dying like the grain of corn in the form they had, to become an authentic word in our own. Words, imagery, silence, all need to be translated, and our praying must give us the opportunity and the sense of obligation to set about it.

20th May

... the alternatives of translation must speak "of worlds different enough to allow the mind space and wonder", must make a virtue, not merely of necessity, but of what has so often been deemed an impossibility. Too often our praying has been locked up in a single idiom, unable to share in a common fire. Within and without our proper tongues we are all required to be translators. Silence, humility, attentiveness, fidelity and imagination, all aspects of spiritual discipline, are involved in such a task. All tongues may declare the wonderful works of God but we need to hear them in our own.

21st May

Prayer is so personal a thing that we cannot presume to share in the praying of other people unless we have lived with them in a personal way, waited on them in silence, and followed the course of their lives. So it is finally with our prayer to God. Our staircase commands no right of entry into His presence, for a personal relation is not achieved like that. All that our efforts can do is to enable us to bring our selves-in-the-making to wait upon Him at the place where he will be to us "as He will be".

22nd May

Péguy took seriously the need to go on learning from his own childhood throughout his life. Descending the ladder meant nothing less than being willing to face the child that you once were, a mystery of humiliation inseparably bound up with hope itself. Like Blake, Péguy revelled in the gaiety of children's games and laughter, but he went further in his respect for the sense of the robust serious purpose of a child growing up in a home where there was always work to be done and shared in. Who but Péguy would have described the mission of Jesus Christ in the picturesque terms of a child being sent to the baker to buy the family's bread, not to stay chattering with the baker but to do the errand and to return?

23rd May

When men and women listened to Jesus of Nazareth speaking, it appears from the records that they were amazed. He spoke in their language, but it was not their own but His. Much of it baffled them, some escaped them, a little remained. The Word took flesh and dwelt among human beings. So is it in lesser degrees with the Word being spoken by poets and others all down the ages.

24th May

These rungs of the ladder today are even more threatened than they were in his time by the devaluation of words that goes on apace. In going apart Péguy took the risk of speaking in ways that would fall on deaf ears or confound even those who endeavoured to listen. The huge 'Cahier' containing the poem Eve with its many thousands of lines, repetitive and slow, dismayed his most much-tried friends. Many dismissed it as mere doggerel. With greater discernment Gide saw the point and said, "What you call repetition is the probing of a man in prayer." Praying has used such a method throughout its history. It is in no sense 'vain repetition' but the use of language to halt the attention while it probes and explores the immensities of its theme.

25th May

In the months before War came Péguy was warning people of the approaching catastrophe, and with a bitter fury commenting upon the power of money to destroy the ancient ties of a people's life. He was reaffirming at ever deeper levels his solidarity with that people, refusing to think of them as the politicians, the professors, the financiers, and the priests appeared to do, holding fast to the conviction that they were even in their most abject poverty of spirit the people for whom Christ died. I believe that in our own praying today, faced by new problems of racial and cultural character, there must be still greater measure of 'turned-towardness' (Martin Buber's word), still more silent listening both to the voices of those in need – every kind of need – and to His voice addressed through them to others. Péguy's attitude throughout was that kind of listening:

> God, I love ever the human voice,
> Voice of departure, voice of sorrow,
> Voice whose prayer often has seemed vain
> Yet plods its way along the weariest road.

26th May

The reckless individualism of four hundred years has gone far to destroy in human hearts a true sense of a people's continuity and common life, substituting for it a fevered nationalism which in its brutality and fearfulness is no more than the swollen egotism of isolated pygmies. Ever and again it must seek a reassurance of itself since it has no real inner life of its own by violent attack upon others. It must be seen to be richer, stronger, tougher than its rivals. What has been largely lost or checked in its growth is the generous fearless outgoing life of the persons who make up the common life open to villages, cities and nations of humankind. Robbed of that, human beings dwindle in spiritual stature, facing bleak destitution, sick unto death.

27th May

We need silence. We need to learn what silence is. We need the time and space which silence alone can provide to get the measure of our secret ladder, to face and not be outfaced by the multitudinous demands of life in the world today. We need to know the kind of silence that makes possible the kind of communication that Pascal hungered for which is communion ... The spirituality we seek must reckon with the mire and clay, the shouting and the torches, the accusations and the mockery. It needs silence to enable it to grapple with that task.

28th May

Men and women whether in the celebration of mysteries or in acts of prayer needed silence to make sense of the words they used, to make room for the unspoken ... Silence alone can provide for both the extremities of our need and the operation of God's grace, permit the insufficiencies of our attention to be checked, and erase the blundering grossness of our insensitive observations. Yet we are far from honouring this necessity in the conduct of our lives.

29th May

The silence Kierkegaard sought was not merely a refraining from words nor was it something to be introduced into a house 'like hanging curtains'. He went on to describe it in the homeliest personal terms, speaking of it as the way in which a woman engaged in creating a home was present in her house. It was unspectacular but pervasive, deliberate but self-effacing, sustained but flexible in its powers of adaptation. Such silence was, he suggested, "like the note, the ground note, which is not made conspicuous; it is called the ground note just because it is underlying." Something quite fundamental to human life depended upon it, something manifest in the earliest and possibly the most influential speechless relationship of a mother and child, something capable of entering into all other relations within the home and of unifying the life of the family in it. "Silence introduced into the house is the homeliness of eternity."

30th May

We need to be silent in order to listen. It is most unlikely that men and women who have grown too impatient to listen to each other will attach importance to listening to God or meaning to the phrase. The loudspeaker threatens to destroy the silent area between one human being and another which Buber has taught us to see as of infinite value in spiritual growth. The devaluation of the word which has so blatantly signalized our times follows hard upon the banishment of silence from our social life. It has been said with justice that it is not so much the gift of tongues that we now need as the gift of ears, not so much the proclamation of our beliefs as the willingness to listen to the ways in which we ourselves are being addressed, not so much the assertion of our knowledge but the silent admission that we are ready to learn.

31st May

... we have been strangely profligate with our talking about God and to Him, forgetting the censure of Jesus of those who supposed that their much talking earned them the right to be heard, and meriting the gibe of yesterday upon "poor talkative Christianity". Not without relief have a great many people now found themselves beyond reach of that institutionalized voice ... [I]n failing to help men and women to use silence well, the Christian Church has added to rather than lightened the burden of lostness, of isolation, of meaninglessness, felt by so many. Its recourse to silence has been too intermittent to make it a supremely important weapon to human beings battling for their lives. We need at all times a solvent of those devices and rigid forms which are imposed upon life, and silence is such a solvent ... The silence that liberates is among the great needs of our time.

JUNE

1st June

Much prayer has wilted and died for lack of silence to enable it to be prayer at all. Prayer without silence becomes a drooling, destructive of the communion sought for, no matter how pious the language it uses. Language without silence is just gossip; gossiping with God is not prayer.

2nd June

We grow up as children of our mother-tongue, learning to use it so easily and so carelessly that its soiled condition, its debasement by corrupt usage, escapes our knowledge and our ability to withstand it. The character of gossip has, with the development of global mass-media so charged the atmosphere that it has been said with truth that "we live in a wind-tunnel of gossip that reaches from theology and politics to an unprecedented noising of private concerns." A lack of, even a deliberate assault upon, reticence has become one of the marked features of our culture. "Our dreams are marketed wholesale." Words, the potential "under-agents of the soul", are made the instruments of corruption, and to dwell among people of unclean lips is, as the Hebrew prophets knew, to be exposed to a contamination that penetrates to the springs of human life ... The steady devaluation of the word in the twentieth century may well prove to be its most fundamental crisis. A new vision of Hell is conjured up in perceiving a state where no-one ceases to talk and no-one listens.

3rd June

All of us need to learn what it means to be of the earth earthy if we are to grow up to our full stature as the children of God. We

cannot, except to our own undoing, ignore or bypass the earth
and the earth-bound ties which God has knit to Himself in love.
To treat His creation as if it were no more than a snare or an
irrelevance is from the outset to defame Him. We shall not learn
to know Him aright, or to honour His name, or to rejoice in His
splendour, if we grow so dull as to fail to perceive how the
heavens declare His glory, or grow deaf to the trees of the wood.
The salvation we look for is, in the terms of the Bible itself, inextricably bound up with the fate and future of all the creation.

4th June

Estrangement from ourselves must squander all our resources in
internal warfare, estrangement from others rob us of our capacity
to become persons at all, but that which divides us from nature
must mean to an ever-increasing extent the loss of a power to
respond, to delight in, to wonder. It must dry up the springs of
worship.

5th June

The soil then was the starting place: soil of the garden planted by
the Lord God in Eden and soil of the fields that men and women
had wrested from the wild earth ever since – back-breaking sweat-
soaked soil; soil of the earth trodden by Christ's feet and by all his
saints and sinners; soil made the scene of His Passion and the
covering of His burial, soil saturated with the tears and blood of
His people down the years; soil the substance of human bodies
moulded to eat and drink and have children, and a marvellous
subtle instrument compounded of clay to respond to the breath of
God; soil of the fleshly house in which God's spirit was pleased to
dwell, and soil to which the body would soon return.

6th June

... when [Péguy] spoke of "a kind of flavour of humanity, a kind
of flavour of earth" that the Son brought back to Heaven, he not
only echoed the cry of delight that old Isaac gave as the smell of
the fields came to him from the supplanter who knelt before him,

but furnished an occasion for joy in the heart of God in tasting the flavour of the earth he had made and the earth His Son had redeemed, supplanting the old Supplanter ... He knew a good deal about detachment and renunciation. They played a great part in the manner of life he chose to follow. He also knew that detachment might mean very little until we had learned first to be attached with the cords of authentic love, that renunciation must have more than superficialities to renounce.

7th June

We stand to lose what the sacramental understanding of life affords if sacraments get detached from the common earth, if that most earth-bound gift of Himself by Christ is severed from field and vineyard, from the labours of men and women in the work of the world. We face such a question that touches the way we pray very deeply, at a time when the fellowship aspect of the Holy Communion has probably gained greater weight of appeal than others, when to some Christians it seems that the social concern has obscured a relation to God, when the emphasis placed upon it may reflect more misgivings about society than a hopeful and brave participation in it.

8th June

A pilgrimage gets to the holy place at last but what gives it its part in prayer is the slamming down of one's feet to complete the journey, praying the while for all its features. A child of that countryside, Péguy trod out the kilometres that brought him at length to the sight of the spire – *le plus beau fleuron dedans votre couronne* – with the joyfulness of a lover, the delight of an artist, the ecstasy of one who worships. The groundwork of his prayer was the rippling ocean of wheat, the bright gold of broom, the dignity of poplars, the gaiety of apple-orchards, the arabesque of the sandy Loire.

9th June

Between Notre Dame de Paris and Notre Dame de Chartres Péguy drew a base line from which to survey all human life, measuring it with his feet as carefully as the Christ had done in His going up and down to the Holy City. The base line of all true vision must be the earth so painstakingly measured out, its inter-section with the Eternal never out of mind, its accumulation of joy and sorrow always in sight. It was the base court of the Holy City and needed to be known as such. Only so would the soil of the earth be rightly used. There is, in Shakespeare's Richard II, a crucial moment when the King puts off his majesty and state to come down to the base court. The King of Kings Himself had so descended, and our ladder of prayer to have any base at all must be located there, on the ground He has consecrated to Himself for ever.

> God bless the ground. I shall walk softly there,
> And learn by going where I have to go.

10th June

Sacramental vision is not instant photography of the world in which we live. It is something learned by the patient education of our sensibility to the engagement of God with the world ... It was a part of Péguy's task to recover men and women to such an awareness of [the] encompassing presence of God. He was well aware that such contemplation was not all that was demanded of the Christian, but he believed that without such a sense of the holiness of the earth he stood upon, he would lose even the will to respond to God. "Why stay we on the earth unless to grow?" Is the dying of the light so trivial a matter that we need not notice it? Is the dawn so commonplace that we can do no more than yawn upon it?

11th June

Do you pray the parish? ... The question is concerned with the way in which we ourselves are related to each other as Christians and as human beings, with the way in which we are all enmeshed in a social life which shapes to a large extent how we live and think and regard each other. It is the world of our assumptions, the world which makes us speak with a certain tone of voice to some and not to others, the world which we take for granted in our scale of values ... We are required to scrutinize and ask questions about this world as deliberately, for example, as some aids to praying direct our attention to the ways in which we dispose our bodies and breathing when we endeavour to pray. What are the marks of this society in which we live? How far is it unified or divided, and upon what basis? In what ways is it oppressive to some, indulgent to others, and why? Who are its deprived and needy, and why are they so?

At this point the parish is the focus of such questioning, that is to say, the immediate nexus of relationships from which we start.

12th June

The parish means a body of people drawn and held together in a spirit that prompts the members to care for, respect and love one another. It is the embodiment in any place of the I-in-You, You-in-Me relationship which Christ prayed for. Larger than the family which has its own special intimacies and responsibilities, the parish so conceived has the job of nurturing all its members that they may, in New Testament terms, grow up to their full stature in Christ. Something begun in the life of the family is to be carried into the next necessary stage of personal development. Small enough to permit a true understanding to grow up between its members, such a body must extend their lives by confronting them with diversities of character and achievements, encouraging each and all to be themselves, relating each to a common life that is enriched by that which each supplies and yet is more than the sum of their gifts.

13th June

Such a body [the parish] would ever be seeking to do two kinds of work; the one within itself in relating its members ever more genuinely to one another in love, the other in shaping a common attitude towards the life of the world in which it is set. Learning to speak the truth together in love, its members would form a community not withdrawn from but actively engaged with the world, and experiencing in an ever-deepening fashion a communion of transcendent character. It would see itself as the Church of Christ, yet be ready to greet and work with others, sharing as far as it could the resources which it possessed. It would at all times be seeking with expectant hope to be able to experience more of the common life in the Body of Christ. Its prayer would be the quite natural breathing of the body thus engaged.

14th June

Somewhere beyond the boundaries of this local church the matters affecting all human life are being considered, pronouncements and reports are being made and commended to the churches, but these are not geared to receive them, not attuned to the job of making them the substance of their prayer and thought. The nervous system of this body transmits such messages feebly, maintains but clumsy continuity of attention, falls back upon pious responses, and gets preoccupied with its own survival.

15th June

The rebirth of the parish as an essential part both of prayer and Christianized life depends to a great extent upon such groups as have been described being ready to see their task in the first place as that of learning a new language, not a language which they invent as the 'in-talk' of a closed circle but a language already being spoken in various tongues throughout the world and which they learn to translate for themselves. They must expect to be puzzled and perplexed as they strive to learn it, and quite dumbfounded by what it implies.

16th June

The groups must learn to think of themselves not as 'study-groups', discussion groups, or prayer circles but as communities of faith setting out like Abraham responding to God to find out for themselves what it means to be growing up to the full stature of the children of God at this time. They will study, discuss, break bread and pray together. They will try to act upon what they see. They will as surely keep contact with other groups of their kind on as wide a basis as possible. There is no reason why the smallest groups should not be open to concerns of a world-wide nature. It is their job to make personal matters of what otherwise will be treated as mere news or information. Through each of them must flow the insights and the strength of the whole Body of which they are part.

17th June

A faith or political commitment that is choked by dead metaphors, slogans and clichés however orthodox can have little part to play in the making of all things new. In Péguy's judgement the curés had lost the parishes because they had imposed such a language on their people, excluding from the sphere of religious devotion those things that were realities of their working lives, disparaging as profane what did not conform to their patterns of piety, thwarting the growth of a common speech that embraced their experience of life with gestures of Christian faith. The outcome in terms of the spiritual life had been a disaster for both. A dumb laity made for an arrogant inwardly-fearful clergy, for a hollowness where communion should have reigned.

18th June

We may not be able to use them [the terms of damnation and salvation] to engage people's attention as we would wish unless we can learn to see them in terms of the future and not of the past, in terms of life and not of an 'after-life', in terms of God to be found ahead as the goal of living and not of God described in the words of a bygone world. A good deal of the shift in theological understanding in our time has been in that direction, a good deal of the perplexity of men and women in religion has arisen from having to turn round and face the future when for centuries they had been accustomed to take their direction from the past. They have repeated 'As it was in the beginning' too many times to take easily to the change, and it is understandable that in the process God Himself seems often to be lost to sight.

19th June

Péguy's political sensitivity fed into his prayer, as the years went on, the evidence of an increasing rejection of personal values, of a steady encroachment on the human aspect of the interests of power and wealth. He saw those communities which had nourished the growth of men and women towards a larger measure of freedom and responsible life subjected to persistent attack. His own response was sharp. His prayer became a militant act, a constant summoning up of spiritual vigilance to withstand and expose the threat of corruption and betrayal.

20th June

... a poem of Edwin Muir entitled *The Refugees* supplies yet another necessary image to the picture, recalling one that belongs by tradition to the Christian mystique, – the refugee Son of Man. To have elevated Him to princely thrones and altars at the expense of His homelessness is to have lost sight of something of profound importance in our understanding of the human condition. Those who are mindful of it eat and drink, buy and sell, marry and give in marriage, and are overtaken by the floods. The Bible could not be more explicit about their case.

21st June

Faced as never before in human history by the need to rethink on a global scale the social and political relations of humankind and to observe them more attentively not only across continents but in the narrower conditions of our factories and cities, it becomes plainer that the problem is spiritual. Such things present themselves as the raw material out of which a new *mystique* must be embodied. They are the primitive soil, *la première argile, la première terre*, to which Péguy as poet was constantly moved to return. They hold promise enough of being fit clay for such enterprise only if the mystique is powerful enough to release the spiritual energy needed for the task of providing in the approaching unification of humankind for the freedom of men and women to grow up as persons.

22nd June

... the clerks of the Church did not appear to realize that a de-christianized society, a world that had learned to do without Christianity, was already here and daily grew more contemptuous of a Church that appeared unwilling to address itself to its real tasks. The battles of both lay and clerical partisans evaded the great problems of poverty and injustice, of community and responsibility. Their invocations of republican or Christian zeal were made only to lend sentimental force to the most hollow gestures. They made no real attempt to deal with a society which forces men and women to live for the sake of production, to produce for the sake of profits, to make profits for the continuance of the process in which the whole world and its resources would be shamelessly exploited. Abdicating their responsibility for the spiritual and moral problems thus created and for the misery inflicted upon the weakest members of society, the clerks contented themselves with a privatized version of Christian faith which handed over a once Christianized France to its sworn enemies.

23rd June

... Péguy was well aware that "the boundary is the best place for acquiring knowledge", and for the exercise of faith and hope. Still more he saw it in temporal terms as the moment of engagement with "the secret event", the profound inward operation which sprang from Christ's going ahead in His world. Freedom meant the ability and willingness of a human being to leave behind all the forms and structures of the past, to make the bet of faith, to risk encounter with chaos, to leap over the walls which offered protection, and to live without the certainties of the past. Prayer was in truth the continual re-committal of a human being to that migrant life.

24th June

The great number [of the Communion of Saints] were as though they had never been. The brief continuance of a name in the mouths of men and women meant very little. What really mattered, what gave joy to a human being, was that out of this unnameable throng a glance, a gesture, a word could by the mercy of God establish a bond of a personal kind, intense and real in this present life and a promise of something greater to be disclosed. With Joan of Arc, this lonely man, Charles Péguy, deeply conscious of sins and out of communion with the Church of his day, knew himself to be in communion with the people of God and with Christ their head.

25th June

Such indeed is the meaning of the communion of the Saints, a fragment of Christian truth too much neglected perhaps today. The more truly we come to understand personal life the more we are learning to see ourselves not standing apart from others but bone of their bone, flesh of their flesh, spirit of their spirit. We are what we share. This communion of saints means also that the enmeshment of our lives is not in some neutral colourless fabric but in an achievement already resplendent with glory to God.

26th June

Péguy knew no less that saints were not men and women of special merit or demigods set between heaven and earth. They were soldiers rather, selected for a particular job, proved warriors in the field, and therefore able to help all those who came into the struggle later. To pray was to participate in their work, their suffering and their joy. Péguy, always a soldier at heart, saw himself drafted into such ranks, not claiming a title for himself, but exultant at being there ... Always it is from the heart of this enlistment that he prays. "We must pray for ourselves in others, among others, in the communion of all." Against the anguish he experienced in his own solitary battles for the truth, he pitted the great "block of holiness" which the saints made up, rejoicing that "in the folds of their cloaks they bore the glory of God and the body of Jesus."

27th June

In the limitations and the achievements of their lives the Saints
spell out for us what it means to be truly human. They fight their
many battles generation after generation with the resources that
seem so pitiful yet prove to be in use indicative of a human
fulfilment beyond all dreams. They are plainly imperfect creatures, they are often defeated and they recover, they deny Him and
they repent, they choke and splutter like a child who is learning to
swim – an image very dear to Péguy – and the Father Himself will
marvel at the triumphant use they make of His gifts.

28th June

Saints are exclamations of delight, the delight of both God and
man. What is more worth marvelling at than the Glory of God
should be so revealed in His creatures? That matter and circumstance compounded into a frail human life should not be, in
Teilhard de Chardin's words "just the weight that drags us down,
the mire that sucks us in, the bramble that bars our way ... but our
accomplice towards heightened being"?

29th June

Saints are part of the language of humanity in its dialogue with
God, the moments of conversation that kindle towards understanding, the evidence that the language of prayer is not an
algebra to be mastered and skilfully put to use but a relation to be
entered into. To grow up unaware of them, to be ignorant of
their diversity of speech, must mean a kind of spiritual disinher-
itance, a human diminishment, a narrowing of our capacity to
communicate.

30th June

Sacred history means much more than the survival of the Chosen
People or the progress of the missionary enterprise of the Church.
It means the disclosure, generation after generation of the pres-
ence of the Saints, of that interpenetration of things human and

divine which Péguy described in the imagery of mortice and tenon, of the appearance among men and women of an interiority giving to personal life a capacity to be other than self-centred, of the energizing of that life by an all-embracing love. Sacred history is, as I have already suggested, wedded to sacred geography, tradition to holy ground, in order that the presence should be located as firmly as possible in time and place, not as a journey's end but as a starting place. When T. S. Eliot writes of Little Gidding in these terms or the more casual visitor of Philip Larkin's poem *Church Going* speaks of

> A serious house on serious earth (it is)
> In whose blent air all our compulsions meet,
> Are recognized, and robed as destinies,

we are confronted by recognition of intimations of transcendence which in Péguy's experience were the evidence of the communion of the Saints.

JULY

1st July

"One never prays apart from anyone ... that would be praying outside the communion." It was manifestly the function of the Saints to assure the man or woman who prayed at some moment of crisis, questioning, strain or joy that they were not alone and that what now appeared to them as an insupportable, meaningless or incommunicable matter could be seen in terms of necessary fulfilment.

2nd July

The more men and women must take into their own hands the shaping of life on the earth and the shaping of themselves, the more acutely are they confronted with contradictions that remain. "You offer God what you have. You offer God what you can." The offering is always incomplete, the doing is always smirched with something less pure than the occasion warrants. You see for yourself that neither your own nor the efforts of all the Saints can be extricated from the sin that attaches to human action.

3rd July

There is ejaculation in a myriad forms; the upward thrust of sap, the fountains overflowing, the quickened pressure of the germ, the steady silent growth of trees, and the passionate leap of courage that the human spirit makes. Péguy's work is itself such a *jaillisse-ment*, an irrepressible exuberance attended by many disconcerting features, but ordered by strong imaginative power. There is at all times a spiritual audacity in his work. He does not falter on the stairs, for having known the depths of misery he hurls himself upwards yet again.

4th July

It still needs saying perhaps that 'mystery' ... means not a puzzle or problem to be solved but a truth which outstretches yet commands the attention of the human mind, defies discovery while it courts it, evokes veneration while it offers itself to be known by the least of its creatures. Mystery breaks into the mental world of humankind unannounced, a hair's breadth dividing its blinding and illuminating power. It embraces God and humanity. In moments of confrontation men and women see and hear – for the senses seem fused into one – some glimpse or utterance of a reality curtained off from ordinary life. To attempt to speak of what they have seen or heard they are forced to use such symbols devised in the deepest levels of their own being as lend themselves to the task. Contradictions persist. Too holy to be spoken of, a mystery compels expression; too vast to be contained in words, it kneads a language to its purpose.

5th July

Religious symbols are needed to give meaning to the continuing presence of mystery in our lives ... The symbol, however inadequately, conveys the numinous experience, the sense of awe, of being confronted by an unbidden unbiddable event, as Jacob was at the ford of Jabbok. It acknowledges something to be adored, it knows exaltation in being caught up in such an experience at all. The line between the conception that we had of ourselves and the world beyond has shifted, the ground on which we stand is changed, we are beside ourselves yet never more truly ourselves than now.

6th July

God is astonished to see how human beings play their parts, astonished to see what His grace can do with them.

With such an expression of divine delight in the virtue hope, Péguy began the *Mysteries of the Holy Innocents* and the *Second Virgin*. *Cette petite espérance* appears in both poems as a little girl, the youngest sister, who causes the old father to cry out with astonishment and joy. "I am not easily astonished," says God, "I am old and have seen much," but He continues to watch this child who darts about, taking her part in processions with her grown-up sisters faith and love, skipping with pleasure, running twenty times further than she need, herself the great promise of life, the sign and seal of the triumph of God's grace ... The past weighs heavily upon humankind, the present is opaque and doubtful, but we are not bound by these; we are the hoper, we are ready to make the leap, we are those people whose grasp of the moment of wonder frees us to go forward.

7th July

Fundamental to Péguy's poetry is the goodness of the creation and God's pleasure in it. Our sins have ravaged it and much brutal insensibility has thrust from sight the wealth of its diversity. Growing unresponsive to it we grow bored with ourselves and one another. Ennui eats out the heart of human enterprise as we fail to grow in a sense of wonder. Péguy's poetry is by contrast a sustained celebration charged with radical amazement at the originality of God. He is always seeing things "as clean and new as on a starting day"; always handling them with an inquiry – what does this mean? what does that do? what part has this played in life? Where does this yield to others? Eternity is plainly too short to finish the enumeration but that is at least how it is best spent.

8th July

Péguy's life was filled on the one hand with all that omnivorous reading gave him, on the other with his own noticing of grain trickling beneath the millstones, a sleeping child's eyelashes resting upon his cheeks, a woman setting down a lamp upon the supper table. It was the immensity of God's providence that kept him utterly astonished. What he set out to do was to help men and women recover a heritage that through ignorance and wilfulness, through pride and folly, had been so roughly squandered. The poet's task was what Vincent van Gogh had once said of his own work – "to put the radiance to human beings that was expressed by the old haloes," but not to human beings only. It meant taking God at His word that "All that I have is thine", and so renewing a world of wonder.

9th July

Péguy had no illusions about the wear and tear of the world:

> Happy is he who remains like a child
> And who like a child keeps
> His first innocence,

but he knew what losses as well as gains had to be endured. He put it starkly enough by saying that the adult could not invent a child's saying, could not even remember it though desperately wanting to do so. "It has vanished from your memory. It is too pure a water and has slipped away from your muddy memory." Yet, he insisted, that saying struck into the adult world like a voice from another creation, from a world where you once were, and as it was heard, you listened to your former soul. Be the fruit what it may, these are the flowers without which there will be no fruit at all. "Before the soul is exalted, it is humbled." Péguy could see no truer humbling in hope than the lives of the children themselves. "Such is my paradise, says God, it could not be simpler. Nothing is less elaborate than my paradise ... children playing in its streets and on the altar steps."

10th July

'Anamnesis' (usually translated 'remembrance') means not the recalling of things past by an act of memory but the re-presentation of things done and said that they may be here and now operative in our midst. It is the heart of the poetic and sacramental understanding of life, the bedrock of Christian faith ... At the centre, at the heart, everything is realized,

> everything is consummated by my Son.
> And it is retold for me.
> And there is a recall, an echo, a reminder
> > and as it were a return.

It was in the strength of that vision that Péguy lived and worked. His intention was always that by learning to pray he and his fellow human beings might come to that centre too.

11th July

Prayer, with its silences and its words, is the supreme form of communication, ever stretching its resources and expending its energy to bring those involved in it more wholly into communion with each other. Addressed to God, it strives to give ever more and more adequate expression to its grasp of reality, to strip off whatever is jargon or cant or cliché, to come clean and make all things new. It acknowledges its own insufficiencies but persists in its intentions. *Toujours l'audace.* "I will speak yet once more." Its importunity presses upon language itself no less than upon time. What is begotten of its consummations is new life for the spirit embodied again and again in new metaphors which are 'lived through', sounded out, and often exhausted by generations of common use.

12th July

Péguy is a man looking at the home in which he has lived and brought up his own family. There is not a thing in it however worn and soiled and broken which has not played its part in their lives together, which is not expressive of their loves and hates, their fears and hopes, which is not sacramental for that reason. *C'est une communion.* Tomorrow the sale may disperse them all, the children may be gone, the bulldozer obliterate the house, but now, in this moment when eternity grips it with eternal Love, there is time to see it bathed in a radiance that is His. There is time, if we so will, for our prayers to handle our own brief bit of this vagabondage. Péguy referred to this human story as "the long remembrance of his vagrancy" in such a fashion that it too may disclose the eternal glory.

13th July

Approfondissement is a descent into the spiritual depths of human experience, below those many distinctions and divisions which human beings have devised for the practical purposes of living, below those serviceable constructions of history, theology, liturgy, poetics, which like all servants tend to become masters, to find the pure potentiality of things, diversity in unity as yet unhardened, unity in diversity exuberant in its wealth. The distinctions are observed, the divisions are erased. "One of the immediate results," wrote Péguy, "is the disappearance of any arbitrary separation of abstract and concrete. The abstract is immediately nourished by the concrete, and the concrete illuminated by the abstract." Péguy's understanding of the Catholic faith was thus rooted in experience of that deep interchange.

14th July

... while Péguy loved those quick flashes of insight, those recognitions of what God was doing which were to him especially French, he was in his own work cautious, deliberate and slow, quite unwilling to permit himself or anyone else to suppose that praying so conceived could ever be anything else but a laborious scouring out of the channels of grace. To our age of speed and instant functioning, Péguy is an impenitent footslogger. He speaks most characteristically when he talks of beginning again. "One is eternally beginning again. Only after the Last Judgement will beginning again come to an end. Prayer is always a beginning over again." To a world excited by its own programmes of planned change and progress it sounds absurd and worse. Yet each of us wants it to be true of ourselves, to be found to be the truth of our life.

15th July

We miss the significance of it if we suppose that we can become onlookers only at such a mystery. Prayer is the necessary recommitment of ourselves to what is being done by Christ in His world, to the pain and suffering it entails no less than to the joy. Exultation in the eyes and mouths of those freed from bonds certainly, but who knows with what pain as the quickened life courses through channels once closed and dead? What bewilderment goes with the first steps of limbs so lately paralyzed?

16th July

In both the *Mystères* the imagery of fatherhood is teased out into an endless variety of playful comments. God is the father who delights in playing with his children, who laughs with them as they lie laughing in His arms, who smiles at the ideas that rattle in their heads like seeds in a pumpkin given to them to play with. His pleasure grows the more as he watches his children learning to play their own game, to take risks, to exercise skill, to make decisions, to play out the play to the end. "I have often played with man, says God, but what a game! It is a game that makes me tremble yet. I have often played with man, but, by God, it was in order to save him. I often play against man, says God, but it is he who wants to lose, the fool, and it is I who want him to win."

17th July

Two generations ago it is doubtful if the idea of prayer and the spiritual life in terms of playing a game or playing a fish – despite the call to be fishers of men – would have gained much favour. It would have seemed to many too flippant a way to approach things sacred and sublime. Play was a matter for the immature, recreation an escape from duties, theatrical playing still suspect. Not many would have been ready to see scientific work in that light either or foreseen the day when Jacob Bronowski would conclude his survey of the Ascent of Man with an account of John von Neumann's theory of games. Even fewer would have welcomed the jester, as the Marxist philosopher Kolakowski does, as one needed to shake our stabilized systems. They had scarcely heard or perhaps forgotten Pascal's words advising them to stop looking for certainty and stability and to prepare themselves to accept the gamble of faith.

18th July

Péguy's praying took on the bet of Christian faith with a seriousness that makes human life threaten to explode at any moment with the revelation of God. "I explode, says God, in plants, in animals, in the beast of the forest, and in man, my creation." Prayer as Péguy then understood it was a matter of learning to live in such an explosive world, of living expectantly. Where so much turns on the bet of faith to be made today, into what depths must we descend to wrest from ourselves such a choice?

19th July

So his praying became the expectant act of one who scans the horizon in hope, the horizon which lies deep in the human soul. 'In depth' has become a commonplace phrase of our time. Men and women have learned to converse about the various strata of being, peered into the abyss, reported the unconscious, made news of the underworld itself. The experts in the field have bored deep into the sources of our human nature, the fierce and often violent unformed stuff of potential spiritual life that has shot up flaming in our midst. The seismic tremors of interior struggles have been charted, the age-old symbols of unconscious impulse catalogued and noted.

20th July

Approfondissement was then the summing up in a single word of all that Péguy as poet and man of prayer was concerned to practise. It may be used to describe what I believe to be the most important task now confronting the Christian Church – as a representative of all humankind – the task of bringing to birth and nourishing a spirituality strong, generous and inspiring enough to help men and women, the world over, to grow up as truly human beings in the immensely complicated world that lies ahead. That spirituality must provide a disciplined way of living in which each person is acknowledged to be needed and contributory to the lives of others, in which the freedom and growth to the fullest possible stature of each is made the concern of all, in which the inner and outer life is nurtured by responsible use of all the resources that humankind has at its disposal; a spirituality which takes its Trinitarian imagery more seriously than ever before, relating the creativity, the humanizing and the unification of humankind in one growing experience of mutual love. The world may well be entering a yet darker dark age than any known before. The demands laid on the spirituality needed during such time will be correspondingly greater.

21st July

The marks of such spirituality were discerned by Péguy. The first is that of amplitude; not the gross multiplication of things but the containment and bearing of the widest diversity of human life within human love. Péguy's imagery was distinctly feminine … "In a generous womb once dwelling" focused the basic conviction upon which all hopes must rest. The Word did, does and will become flesh and dwell among men and women. Humankind needed to learn all over again the character of expectation which it once symbolized in Christ's mother … The wisdom of the body, the wisdom of the heart, had to be listened to. The brooding over the yet unformed had to be repeated if the miracle of creativity were to continue in time. "Creativity is always linked with the happy moment when all conscious control can be forgotten." "According to thy word" spelled out the essential truth. The meaning of the word "present yet not present" required an amplitude of spirit, humbled to its task, joyful in its expectation of mutuality and diversity, ungrudgingly welcoming of what must be infinitely costly. Amplitude waited upon intimations of transcendence, and made room for them.

22nd July

The second feature must be that of imagination. The needed spirituality must be freed on the one hand from dead externalized imagery which can only enslave the minds of men and women and make them fearful and cruel in turn, and sensitized to a new and deeper awareness of all that art and poetry can make known to us of our spiritual stature and our engagement with God. The imagination of the poet is needed to hold together "the mighty opposites" that we must face in living, for where it is lacking we project our fears of the uncontrollable world, within and without ourselves, upon those dwelling with us. "The displaced person today is a pathetic image of the illness that has befallen our body social, namely its inability to tolerate diversity without undue anxiety." *Approfondissement* meant nothing less than a new resolution of ancient issues appearing in as yet unrecognized guise.

23rd July

... while needing the help of artists and poets to carry us boldly to new rungs of the ladder, we must learn also to act imaginatively with one another in the families and groupings into which we come or are drawn. An imaginative process was needed, a cultivation of the garden of souls, not dependent upon one leader or an élite or an ecclesiastical ministry, but "compacted by that which every part supplied." A cultural solidarity continually refreshed by imaginative effort of all those who participated in it would be the true basis for new ventures of faith.

24th July

The third feature was that of fidelity. The word rings through all that Péguy wrote, and he used it as the touchstone of every decision he made in politics or family affairs or intellectual work. He deprecated turning it into something heroic and preferred to speak of it in terms of a craftsman choosing a piece of wood for the job to be done. It was matter of fact and infinitely costly. Any English parish priest who has worked in a working-class parish will have heard it said of someone's facing of that kind of decision, "He had it to do." It is not resignation or apathy but a considered sense of responsibility, of fidelity to the calling of being human.

25th July

The fourth feature; a freedom of spirit that makes us most like God in whose image we have been formed. It makes us also concerned with the liberation of all who are oppressed or enslaved. What Péguy understood in terms of *approfondissement* here was a continual searching out of all those things which denied or curtailed the freedom of men and women. It meant unwearied observation to catch sight of those "whom Satan hath bound", to hear the pleas of those who had no voice to make themselves heard.

If we fail to hear the prayers of men and women for such liberation, how can we be free as a matter of grace?

26th July

The fifth feature confronts us with the costliness of it all. *Approfondissement* makes it clear that the pain and suffering does not grow less. The hidden underside of all Péguy's mysteries is itself the mystery of pain ... In the depths he cried out his own *de profundis*, in the heights his own *Te Deum*, and both were infinitely rich. But their quality was nowhere more truly disclosed, more humanly expressed, more spiritually charged, than in the moments of *approfondissement* that he used to attend to what fatherhood meant to him. He returned to it again and again, passing steadily from one level of perception to others. Who knew anxiety like the father of a sick child? Who gave hostages to fortune like the father of a family? Who hoped that his life's work might bear fruit like a father working for his children?

27th July

A poem or even a single line of poetry needs more than one person's lifetime in which to yield its meaning. Not only what the poet intended but the reverberations of what he wrote, which come echoing from the circumstances of other times, are full of meaning for us now. Whispering or bellowing in our ears they surge around our lives today, and tomorrow will beat upon other shores. Now, when the night sky of the Lord is upon us, we must ask as did Isaiah long ago: "What of the night?" (Isaiah 21.2)

28th July

Whether remaining obstinately separate or determinedly seeking assimilation the Jew has therefore always aroused disquiet. Laurens van der Post has written of this age-old problem in his novel *The Seed and the Sower*. He speaks of "the mass instincts to seize an excuse for pulling down the very thing that they themselves have need of elevating", and of those who appear to be predestined to bear the suffering that this brings because they "personify most clearly the singularity that has to be humiliated and sacrificed." The Jew has been throughout history that humiliated brother.

29th July

Each of us has a share in the shaping of what is said and done in the world. Here each of us bears some witness to truth or betrays it. Indifference or unthinking acquiescence in things as they are or as we suppose them to be, even our silence at critical times, contributes to what takes place.

30th July

Judaism has been summed up as constituting unceasing interrogation. For both Jews and Christians, being alive to God must mean being sensitive to the fact that his questions are being put to them. It is a function of the Spirit as Jews and Christians have known it to enter searchingly into the human house, and there to put questions, now like a breath and now like a wind, to try all things that it finds there, to question their fitness to endure. The process in our own night-sky is of near gale-force winds.

31st July

It is a delusion to suppose that the disturbing questions will, if ignored, go away, if suppressed be forgotten, or that by hiding ourselves like naked Adam we can escape them. It is no less delusive to expect that we shall get comforting answers to our own questionings. To live with our uncertainties is not simply a necessary part of our education at all levels; it is the very truth of faith. To endure the sifting process of interrogation is the hallmark of discipleship.

AUGUST

1st August

The Holocaust is not to be separated from the long record of the persecution of heretics, the burning of witches, the torture of prisoners, the starving of peasants and artisans, the massacre of minorities, and the slower but equally anguish-producing insensitive treatment of women and children that went on at all times.

2nd August

To ask the right questions has long been seen to be the foundation of all fruitful advances in knowledge. To hear what questions are put to us has marked true wisdom. It is our business, as men and women who are concerned to grow to our full stature, to be alive to such questioning by God and humanity. We must sort out what questions we should ask and hear, cease asking foolish ones, and in no way flinch from those that are rightly searching; we must distinguish those that call for a solution from those that need only answers, and dwell patiently with those that await revelation.

3rd August

After the acceptance of Christianity as the official religion of the Roman Empire, Christ had been portrayed as the Pantocrator, from whom imperial authority devolved. The icons of Emperor and Christ were virtually indistinguishable; such clothing of Christ in purple was acceptable to one age and an offence to another. It had been done before and would be done many times again. And, how could Christ's own clothes be put upon him?

4th August

Today when the nations lurch in uncertain fashion towards the one world that their many achievements make possible, we must turn to the basic suggestion of Israel's faith with new force. It is the faith of a people for ever marching, a people of tents rather than a Temple, a people learning to read God's law in their hearts, a people committed to giving the stranger welcome, facing a new world with a deep trust in God. Our task today is the recovery of what is essentially a Jewish concept of humanity's destiny.

5th August

Christians have at all times made the Jews the image of their own self-estrangement. Modern Europe, still half Christian, inherited and redoubled the hatred as it grew more conscious of cracks running through the social and personal fabric of its existence. The Jew is always the brother rejected, the brother cast into the pit or sold as a slave. The Jew is the man or the woman deprived of the dignity of a human being, the despised and rejected, the wretched of the earth. Evil's mockery was at its height when people were goaded to burn and to murder Jews 'after the flesh', when they failed to see the humanity of their fellow human beings whom they destroyed. The Holocaust happened because human beings had come to such depths of self-loathing that only the destruction of humanity could offer relief.

6th August

An age-old question presses on the consciousness of humankind, a question compounded of others formulated by the Jews long ago. What does it mean to be human and what does God require of us? The human response made to the Divine demands, as Israel understood them, has been a melancholy chronicle of mutiny, folly, evil devisings and fears, though enlightened by some snatches of beauty and goodness and a turning again in tears. There have been times in Israel's own history when the light has been utterly darkened ... but stubborn Jewry still holds to its faith before the world to remind humankind that its appointment is with a living God.

7th August

... with the beginnings of the persecution of those who held different views and religious beliefs, in the first instance in the persecution of the Jews, the Christian Church embarked upon a course which steadily weakened its spiritual authority. It deprived itself of the authority of love and made way for the time when secular powers could outdo it in strength and expose its weakness to a world where brutality reigned.

8th August

Both faiths have in their liturgies acknowledged the message of dust. Ash Wednesday today has hardly the place which Yom Kippur holds for the Jews. All Souls' Day likewise lacks profundity of attention. Good Friday is swallowed up quickly in Easter. A new start must be made today by men and women of both faiths to learn from the ashes now lying on Europe's soil what God, the One God and Father of both, requires them to learn together. It is not only 'the humanism of the European Jew' that lies in the dust but that of Christian Europe too.

9th August

The very degree of the objectivity of the word 'mystery' as something which holds things known and unknown together in a bond of faith has been the most satisfactory aspect of its use.

10th August

That Christ now appeared in imperial style, crowned, sceptred, robed and enthroned, made clear what relations were to obtain in the future. Christianity now had a political aspect inextricably bound up with its theological definition. For some time the Jews were able to thrive, but they lived henceforth in the shadow of the Cross, preserved, it was said, to be converted, in practice to be spurned and hated.

11th August

The Jesus we seek is always striding on ahead of us. The Gospels themselves are insufficient. They point to things unsaid, to things which they encourage us to expect, to things which lie beyond yet have bearing upon our innermost life and the world we live in. But their insufficiency is entirely right. They are signposts and not destinations. They demand that greatest of God's gifts – imagination – if they are to bring us any distance along the road of which he is both the way and the goal.

12th August

Do Christians really believe that what has been said so far is all that needs to be said and that it has been said in the only possible way, that it must do duty for all time? Is it conceivable that what was said in good faith years ago may today be a stumbling block, a barrier of words, to hinder men and women – and not Jews alone – from hearing and seeing Him for themselves? May it be that Jews can help Christians today to look once again at Jesus himself and see him with new eyes?

13th August

The train-loads of Jews on their way to the death-camps passed through countrysides dotted with Christian spires. There were churches not very distant from the camps where Jews were gassed and burned. Those spires were symbols of a faith whose adherents were largely insensitive to the fact that that faith had sprung from the impact of the life of one Jew upon the world, and still more insensitive to any sense of relationship to Jews who had grown up in their cities and towns.

14th August

Hebrew 'knowing' is the total response to the one whom it claims to know. It finds consummation of being in its self-giving to the one who is known. Hence it is often in terms of sexual union such as inspired the Song of Songs that it is expressed, but it transcends that relation too. It came to speak rather of friendship as its supreme description of Abraham and Moses in relation to God. It appears again in the words of Jesus to the disciples in John 15.15, "I have called you friends", and carries the implication that they are called to participate in the love with which God loves us, the love that is within the Godhead itself.

15th August

The medieval world-picture has vanished because men and women have changed their manner of life and the picture no longer fits. What has failed to arrive is a post-Christendom working hypothesis in which a Christian supernatural history makes full use of what modern historical learning affords. We are still in an uneasy phase in which ecclesiastical history is offered instead ... Religion needs to be ... nourished by the scientific, that it may become the kind of history that can be prayed by men and women summoned by God to stand on their feet in the world God has made.

16th August

The final statement of the Second Vatican Council could in fact be said to represent one more triumph for ecclesiastical history in that it did little to provide an unequivocal rejection of the ancient charge of deicide made against the Jews, and still less to condemn the anti-semitic persecution that had sent millions to a horrible death. It contented itself with deploring what had happened; not even this resolution was passed without opposition.

17th August

We cannot however lose sight of the fact that the Holocaust's lesson is that without a quite different historical vision men and women will not behave in a radically different way. The task committed to Christians and Jews is one in which both help towards the shaping of world history written as it were in the presence of God, a *Civitas Dei* for humankind today.

18th August

It was the prophets who recognized and drove home the point that
the health of this nation turned on the choice between true and
false religion. True religion, true service of God, lay in the up-
holding of the life of the community in just and merciful treatment of all creatures, human and animal.

19th August

The essential Hebrew message as to the meaning of history was
not changed by the coming of Christ but carried to its universal
dimension. In the face of the seemingly all-powerful Roman
Empire, the predominance of Graeco-Roman culture, and a
corrupt self-destructive régime in Judea, Jesus brought into
being the nucleus of the world-wide community that was to be.
How baffling yet how compulsive His work was is clear in the
Gospel record. Being utterly faithful to Israel's calling could at
this point be openness towards humankind. The Samaritan, the
Roman, the outcast, the despised, were there to be met as brothers. Jesus called his disciples 'friends' not servants because they
were meant to understand his work and to embody it in their
own flesh. They were to address themselves fearlessly to the
whole world without letting go of a particle of God's truth
revealed to the Hebrew people.

20th August

That sense of history was lost as the Jewish element in the
Christian community sank into insignificance. Accepting the
status of official religion in the Roman Empire it exchanged its
fellowship life for the organized structures of a religion. Very
soon it expressed its despair of the world by turning to a two-
standard version of Christian life, elevating the life of with-
drawal from worldly affairs to be the supremely virtuous way. It
transferred human attention and hopes towards another world in
the heavens and drained human history of all significance save
that of securing a passport to life hereafter. With that dualist out-

look the Church strove and failed to control human life. The world thus despised took revenge and steadily degraded the Church, using it when it thought fit to do so, ignoring it when it pleased.

21st August

Unwanted commodities, unfashionable models, brands out of favour, go for scrap and in efficient economies are re-cycled to provide materials as well as room for their successors. Marx did not believe that humankind could be treated thus. The whole motivating force of his life's work was a passionate protest against it. His picture of men and women as commodities, like that of Jeremiah's pots, served as an illustration of a searing vision. His aim was to challenge the contemporary practice of humankind which reduced men and women to the condition of 'things'. How to expose the nature of that practice in theoretical terms was the task to which he devoted his life.

22nd August

The relations of men and women thus set to work were function-al and impersonal, designed to exclude whatever did not con-tribute directly and narrowly to the job. It was a picture of human life quite insufficient to answer the question What is Man? ... but it showed how the question was being dealt with in practice. While 'Cotton was King' men and women were his slaves – the psalmist's description of God-given glory was wholly beside the point. Marx savagely documented what the point was – that whatever men and women might be in themselves or to God, in the working relations of economic life they were hands at the looms, pens in the counting-house, genitals in the stud farms, breeding slaves to sell in the states of the American Deep South.

23rd August

'We must find humanity again' becomes therefore the search for our fellows in the tower-blocks and the shanties, in the owner-occupier estates, inner-city streets, in villages and ghettoes. We must seek men and woman in relationships – marriage and love – in the fears of the sick and the guilty, in the meanings and losses of meaning that overtake and dismay. Auschwitz is not to be separated from the total condition of people's lives in the world today. It is to be seen much more as a fearful despairing rejection of what it means to be human, the frenzied attempt of dehumanized men and women to destroy rational thought and human relations. It was supremely a gesture of self-loathing. It expressed contempt for all and everything that humanity is or does.

24th August

God comes to and deals with human beings, reveals and makes himself known as a man would do with his friend, and as heart can speak to heart. God does not possess or use the prophet in an impersonal way, but rather kindles the spark within him, stimulates the whole soul to action, enables the human being to speak for God.

25th August

Happy indeed are those who love and believe themselves to be loved, but the shadows of turning lie thick across human paths. What shall we do when God, man or woman, delight us no longer or when meaning itself has seeped out of life?

26th August

... We must be made deeply aware of the disturbing demand made upon our religious life by this summons to move. The Exodus was no incident of past history, nor was Abraham's call an interesting event in the life of a nomadic people. Both were moments of divine intervention, announcing a new phase of life "to the Jew first, but also to the Gentile" (Rom.2.10): both were part of a chain reaction to be followed through in the history of humankind demanding that in each generation men and women be awakened to the need to forego the spiritual comfort so easily provided by religion and to prepare themselves for the next stages of their long march.

27th August

The practice of Christian devotion has owed much to its Jewish
springs. It found no better pattern for its liturgical prayer than
Israel's recalling of participation in the life of a covenanted Body
of God's great saving acts, release from bondage, feeding of the
flock, forgiving of their sins, directing of their hopes towards the
Day of His Coming. It found no better means of sustaining and
training the spiritual life than by using the Jewish scriptures, especially the Psalms, and adding to them its own distillation from
Biblical sources in Canticles of its own. It took over Hosannas,
Hallelujahs, Glorias to give voices to ecstasy in prayer. From the
deepest of all wells it drew the Lord's Prayer. Its use of Amen gave
a firm foundation to words and silence alike.

28th August

An extraordinary marriage of Jewish inspiration with felicitous
English prose, begot in the sixteenth century a style of making
melody to the Lord in words that continued to echo through the
work of novelists and poets long after many of them had turned
away from the Church. Hardy's poetry is inconceivable apart
from the Psalmody of the Book of Common Prayer, an authentic
continuation of the ironical and passionate questioning of Israel's
God which down the ages has found its way into the prayer books
of the Jews.

29th August

I have listened to Rabbi Gryn describe what going with his father,
mother and brother to Auschwitz was like, how the millions died
and the few survived, how he kept Yom Kippur in his prison
camp, how feeling he was already dead as a human being he
nonetheless prayed the liturgical prayers of his people and asked
for forgiveness, crying his whole soul out and learning that God
was also crying. Bearing in mind that at this moment millions of
men and women drag out their lives in similar misery, how dare I
do other than try to pray as he did? Auschwitz, said Rabbi Gryn,
is about Man and his idols. It is about abominable things set up in

place of God. This brilliant powerful, clever, sophisticated world of ours stands so nearly in the grasp of inconceivable Evil and time is so short that no other talk can compare in urgency with this. In a quite special sense the ancient biblical choice of Life against Death is ours today. We make the choice only by learning to pray, by turning to God.

30th August

In attending my parish church I do not hear my attention drawn to the fact of Auschwitz week after week so that along with fellow-Christians I am compelled to think and pray about it. The fate of the Jewish people in modern Europe is not connected with the crucified Jew who appears in the stained-glass window above the altar. Newspapers tell me and those around me that Jews are a political nuisance in today's world. History tells me that they have through the ages been an ethical nuisance too. But how then are they to be prayed for? The problem of human suffering is never far from the hearts and minds of the congregation but no one speaks of the significance of the suffering of His people or suggests that something must be done about it. The reality of Israel's vocation to suffering, if one may dare to speak of it in that way, is accorded not the silence of awe but of disregard. It interrupts no habitual practice, challenges no customs, wounds no conscience. No one cries out, "Give your whole attention to this." There is no one day in the Church's year when Christians feel obliged to come together to weep for our sins against the Jews.

31st August

The gas ovens that burned human bodies could be, under God, redemptive did they also burn up fantasies and false dreams of the world we have known. But it depends upon whether we see the task as a 'burning question' for ourselves too or whether we wait for the ashes, the ashes of death, to settle upon us.

SEPTEMBER

1st September

To be holy today means seeking anew the engagement point with this environmental God. No generalized devotion or piety can be substituted for the particular response it calls for, since this would miss the point that God's work, like that of the artist, is unique and specific hour by hour, is in motion like the stars and the winds, and that praying must have the fine point of a moving pen.

2nd September

The Greeks ask, "What is good?" The Jews ask, "What does God require of thee?" From these questions flowed two different conceptions of life. For the Jew to be human meant finding out and observing the requirements of God with all the zest of a lover till the scope of requiredness embraced creation itself. So to the Jew first but to the Christian also the primary task of prayer was a resetting of sights from day to day to ascertain what the requirements of God were in a world which moved towards a new world-order and common life, a world whose dazzling achievements called for not only great intelligence but for a still greater measure of charity.

3rd September

The process of transmutation can scarcely be other than painfully experimental. What matters is that the process should go on, that the Spirit should be at work in these unwelcoming fields, that the words to express what is sought should be found. It is the business of prayer to try to penetrate to the reality of human experience. Reality should be known, and prayer must endeavour to hold it to God.

4th September

Auschwitz marks a crisis for the attempt to face reality, not only
for Jews but also for Christians. This may have been recognized
by certain leaders of Christian thought, but it is not something
that has made an impact upon the prayer life of the Church. The
reason is painfully obvious. The great bulk of Christian congregations have lived so long without feeling any need to acquaint
themselves with Jews and their history that Auschwitz does not
have any great bearing upon their lives. Religion has actually
insulated them from any possible sense of pain arising from what
has happened. Without some new effort to establish a relationship of concern enlightened theologians will have little effect.
Congregations will go on using the Bible and singing the Psalms
and Canticles without realizing that a new and greater degree of
unreality has been added to what they do.

5th September

... in prayer the Jew participates in a relationship established
between God and His people of quite vividly intimate character.
The personal aspect of prayer is in no way diminished; it is raised
to true dignity and vastly extended by being set in the context of
God's dealings all down the ages with His people ... Since Israel
has not been permitted to forget the terms of its Exodus calling,
its prayer carries with it the full weight of community purpose.
Christian liturgical prayer has preserved community language but
rarely succeeded in matching it with the shared life in the Body of
Christ. Hence it has not been able to withstand the encroach-
ments of the spirit of individualism fostered by modern life.

6th September

A *Yom Ha'Shoah* liturgy was planned for Christians in 1972. It con-
sisted of readings from diaries, poems and novels written during
and after the years of the Holocaust together with choruses and
prayers. It sought to allow the voices of the victims themselves to
be heard; thus we stand with them, and Christians can know
themselves to be the survivors, spared by the mercy of God and

compelled to ask what He would now have them do. "Help us to
hear the voices which you send today." Grant that we do not forget them. God Almighty is called upon "to raise up a man who
will go peddling through the world", that familiar Jewish peddler
who will offer the cakes of soap that a million lives have been
destroyed to make, a peddler who will disturb the conscience of
humankind, bring into our streets and homes and council cham-
bers and churches the reek of the concentration camps, bring to
our ears the screams and weeping of mothers and children, old
men and boys, bring us to a halt in the midst of an otherwise for-
getful life. Dare we protest and plead to be left undisturbed?
Auschwitz assembled millions of outstretched hands because
those of Jesus of Nazareth had left us unmoved.

7th September

The Church's liturgical forms were too anatomical, wondrous
structures indeed, but with bones of theology that lacked the flesh
and blood that life in the world should supply. Its hymns and its
canticles were fixed in traditional modes. All too rarely a poet
broke through the accustomed forms and grasped theological
truth in words that gave it an imaginative power. Writing of the
Vexilla Regis hymn, David Jones said tersely: "It is the sort of thing
that poets are for; to redeem us is part of their job." We likewise
need new poetical forms to continue that work of redemption.

8th September

The two things that a changed style of praying call for are: a new
vision of the involvement of Christianity with the history of
humankind and a new readiness to use poetry, drama, dance,
music and all the arts to express what this involvement means. At
the moment a Christian congregation is likely to be unaware of
the tumultuous majesty of the scene in which it is called upon to
play a part. It hugs its accustomed paths and forms and sees little
or nothing of either abysses or mountain tops. Its glimpses of
green pastures get more vague and conventionally tricked out. Yet
this impoverishment in our churches is the outcome of choice, of
a standing aside from the historical, interrogative and lyrical

participation in a vast cosmic drama into which God has called His people.

9th September

Judaism still lives in the world despite all the efforts of demonic men to destroy it, because it has never abandoned a willingness to begin again. Chaim Potok's words at the opening of the novel *In the Beginning* are precise: "All beginnings are hard." They get harder the more we are led to make them in fundamental matters of faith and commitment and self-knowledge. Whether it is a new way of understanding the Bible or ourselves, all beginnings are hard – "especially a beginning that you make by yourself," that is, the effort to think and to pray and live in a new direction. Rebirth was the Gospel's description of it. Dying daily was to give new scope. What the churches are faced with today is no less a momentous choice.

10th September

... as for the Kingdom of God, how seriously do we in public and private prayers and in our discussions about the life of faith set the Kingdom of God at the heart of all? Does it mean that much? Do we even pause as we say, "Thy Kingdom come"? We speak of it as a world hereafter. A few still believe it to mean the Church. More rarely do we come across those who await its coming on earth. The lead-story of the Gospels, that the Kingdom of God is at hand, is not news for most Christians today. It has no significant place in the way they look at the world.

11th September

What has not been uppermost then in Christian theology, practice and prayer has been a joining together of personal involvement in building the Kingdom on earth and a sense of the part this great hope has played in human history until now. Thus it has neither impressed itself deeply upon the minds of worshippers of God that the Work of the Kingdom is something of daily concern, nor has it enabled them to look at this history of humankind, in hopeful but realistic terms. Much of that history has been compounded of idealized versions of the work of the Church and servile attention to the Powers of the World.

12th September

That many brave Christians risked their lives to help Jews must be gladly declared, but in so far as the Holocaust's lesson is unmarked by churches, church leaders and the great mass of churchgoers there is no reason why the same evils should not be repeated. Unless that lesson is learned, it will be easier to repeat evils, for the credibility and integrity of the Church is so weakened by what has been done that without metanoia, the searching of soul, it will have less resistance to offer.

13th September

In Jewish understanding of the Kingdom of God men and women were not subjects ruled over by and at the whim of an inscrutable despot but witnesses to and co-partners with the Lord God whose purpose all things were designed to show ... It is always coming, always 'not yet' achieved in its fulness and beauty, for its reality does depend on and must wait for the true response of love coming-to-be in human hearts. It cannot be brought into being by fiat or imposition.

14th September

For too long Christianity has connived at the destruction of Jewry, whether by outright murder or by missions. If we are startled at finding these two things set together, it may help us to see how both have hindered the Kingdom's coming.

15th September

We mistake Israel's role in human history if we fail to see it as what has been called 'a system of communication'. Just as the language of great poets, the music of composers, the drawing of artists, the plans of architects and the skills of many others extend, embody and nourish the human spirit, it has been Israel's task to compose, define, celebrate, give form to, the true community, the right relationships of men and women in society, to be a holy nation. The pattern which Israel has been required to seek to honour down the ages is that of humankind growing up to its true stature.

16th September

... in 1840 the Jews of Damascus, men, women and children, were arrested and tortured at the instigation of the French consul and of the Governor of the city, allegedly for murdering a Capuchin friar to secure blood for ritual purposes. All Europe soon learned what had taken place, and though the French Government under Thiers defended its consul, the outcry was of sufficient force to enable leading Jews like Adolphe Crémieux from France and Moses Montefiore from England to visit Turkey and to secure by personal intervention the release of the prisoners. The Damascus affair showed, as did the Dreyfus trial fifty years later, that popular Christian feeling could be whipped up into hysterical outbursts against the Jews to a point where rational behaviour could be swept aside. The point was not lost on Heine who saw it as a brief disclosure of powers that could be loosed to annihilate humanity itself.

17th September

Human beings have always been ready and adept to build up walls within and without their minds to defend themselves, to exclude others, to wall up nations and their own souls. China's Great Wall would be the only human erection perceived by eyes from another planet. Perhaps more penetrating vision might see the wall of partition designed to exclude the Jews as something more symbolic of the human condition, something which throws darkness across this world as nothing else has done.

18th September

... if we look to Jesus, the Fourth Gospel, a book by no means tender to the Jews, records Him as saying that salvation was of the

Jews. This suggests that we too must seek Him among His own people and not claim that because some of them cast Him out, He was parted from them for ever. Israel's God was not only the God who had chosen this people but the God who had said that He would not let them go. They were graven upon the palms of His hands. To seek Him elsewhere would be to run the risk of being beguiled by Christs of human making, by Christs of much theological subtlety. The obvious difficulties of Christian work in the world today sprang from just such confusion of mind, from this image of a Christ detached from His people. Pious imagination sinks into vain imaginings unless checked by constant reference to the Jesus whose flesh was Jewish.

19th September

If the Holocaust is to do for humankind what the story of Joseph in Egypt suggests, what the Passion of Christ exhibits, we must see the evil for what it is ... Words – Holocaust, genocide, mass-murder – can blur the sharp image of that which the eyes of the spirit must see. But we must try to comprehend the incomprehensible, the men with a hatred of life, of love, of light, with a hatred of all that is human and divine, who desired the darkness and death of the spirit itself. Egyptian records tell us nothing of Joseph, Roman history has scarcely an unassailable genuine word on the Passion of Jesus. Our news-service is better. The facts have been told to the world. Our danger lies not in our lack of knowledge but in our not knowing what they meant and must mean today. To miss out on that is to share the fate of Hitler's victims.

20th September

The historical fact of the Christian Church in no way annulled Israel's calling to sanctify God's name in the world. No one could ever usurp that role. It was time that Christians affirmed it and ceased to look upon Jews as unaccountably stubborn in maintaining the ancient faith. It was time too that Jews learned to recognize that the covenanted relationship of God and humanity had been opened to all humankind and that the Christian Church must win men and women through Christ to participate in it.

21st September

The tragedy of the past nineteen hundred years lies in the separation of these brothers [Jew and Christian]. The Holocaust must
bring home to them both that only through mutual recognition of
each other with no other motive but that of love may they play
their appointed part in the world's redemption. Now is the time.
Christianity has come perilously near to accepting the kingdoms
of Church and State in lieu of seeking the Kingdom of God. The
Jew has come near to thinking that outside the Jewish there is no
valid consciousness of the world.

22nd September

In Egypt, the story says, it was through interpreters that Joseph
first spoke to his brothers. Revelation waited until he could speak
with them face to face in their common tongue, till their souls
were ready to hear at the deepest levels of need. Interfaith dialogue is likewise a matter of personal recognition, not easily
arrived at but to be sought for with tears. It calls for much greater
awareness of what the relationship asks of and offers to men and
women than has yet been commonly understood. True religion
means not the exalting of spirit, nor the mystical vision, but a
response to being sought out and addressed ... It is time that they
learned to keep watch together.

23rd September

"By far the greater part of what is today called conversation
among men and women," Buber wrote, "could be more properly and precisely described as speechifying." The speeches
belonged to a world of slogans and cynical rhetoric, of
newspeak and doubletalk. The telecommunication medium was
about to reinforce the one-sidedness of public utterance. Few at
that time could have guessed at the extent to which true communication was threatened. Thomas Mann left Germany to
assert the writers' responsibility for human values expressed in
language, believing, as Buber did, that the death in the pot of
the German régime was not simply the vile brutal treatment of

men and women but also the falsification of speech, the devaluation of words, the corruption of language, which destroyed the relations of persons. The dehumanization of political life was projected in words that brought darkness to a whole people.

24th September

What then was dialogue? It might mean an exchange of views, chance conversation, inquiry or flirtation. It could be as famous as the dialogues of Plato, as studied as the imaginary conversations devised by men of letters, as infamous as conspiracies to murder. In Hebrew usage it meant the expression of the most profound relationship in terms of the Spirit. It was that which both prophets and psalmists knew, as they themselves were drawn into the purging and quickening of this expression. It was in itself a manifestation of God's love for His people that such dialogue could take place. "They shall hear my voice," and in hearing and answering they would become truly His children. It was what the Johannine Gospel implied by the 'I-in-You, You-in-Me' community of being. It was not bounded by words or times or places, but being entered upon partook of the boundlessness of God and confirmed humanity's creaturely existence.

25th September

Now, at this moment, God speaks and is heard by those who are attentive, who face creation as it happens. It happens as speech directed precisely at them. The test of all true religion lies in its ability to help us to hear ourselves so addressed, and to hear beyond Joseph's voice and the voices of brothers the One who speaks through the moments of meeting, whose voice is that of rebirth.

26th September

Buber minimized nothing of the contradictions that set Christian and Jew apart. The lines must be drawn not in hatred but love. What was called for was the artist's approach, not commanding but coaxing the form of it into light. It meant being humble enough to rejoice in the otherness of the brother, in the singular otherness to be loved. To the two faiths fell the one task.

27th September

The real questions that the Holocaust should raise can be distorted or hidden away from us by the imagery we are led to use. The word Holocaust itself is suspect. The reality we must face can impose too great a burden on our sensibility, so that we fall back on words and images that are already worn and dulled. We have no language adequate to our need. We are outraged by the event, we feel constrained to speak, but how can we speak of the unspeakable? The words take over and in using them so often we cease to think or go on thinking about the significance of the event. The occasion slips away. Yet now, more than ever, it is important not to let ourselves be seduced from the fundamental task imposed upon us.

28th September

What is it that we have learned? Is it more than a hope or resolution that Christians and Jews should now begin to be 'nicer' to each other than they have managed to do for almost two thousand years? If more, then how much more? What does the 'more' involve? In this book we have looked briefly at a number of things that are called 'religious', such as the Kingdom of God, the question of prayer, the differences that historically divided Jews and Christians, the concept of humanity that has been influential in our respective cultures. Do we see these things as being of supreme importance for the future of humankind, for our children's children? Is it conceivable that in failing to take them more seriously than we did in the past we have doomed generations to come to a bloodier and more cruel fate than even the victims of Auschwitz knew? In other words, does it matter so much how we stand before God? Are we convinced that radical change in Christian thinking, behaviour, teaching, church life and mission will be needed if Christianity is to do more than repeat the sad spectacle of the churches of Europe looking helplessly, tongue-tied, on the triumph of Evil spelled out in the murder of Jews?

It is because I believe this to be supremely the religious question that faces us and one that is even now gathering weight and momentum to give it an urgency we dare not neglect, that I take up the metaphor of the eclipse of God. Simply to use it gives no guarantee that we use it rightly but use it we must.

29th September

Eclipse … suggested the darkening of once bright skies. This was fond delusion; the darkness had always been there. It was our artificial lights that flickered or were extinguished. As soon as we could we lit them again, lit even more brilliant lights. We kindled those lights "brighter than a thousand suns" and cast the shadow of Hiroshima round the world. We took pains to develop the bright art of the film and television screen to extend our vision to seemingly infinite lengths. We brought into every home the shades of the black and merciless things that crouch in our streets, the darkness that falls across the relations of men and women, the fading out of beliefs that were charged to give an assurance of light.

30th September

Theology … has frequently used such terms as the death, the disappearance, or the eclipse of God. His silence, His hiddenness, His whereabouts, have all been studiously discussed. It is more common to speak of Him in the depths than in the heights. We have repeated Pascal's words with a new respect as our cosmological knowledge has extended the picture of the dark immensity of the Universe in which we live. We perceive a little more surely the brief nature of the play in which we perform our parts. We are not unaware of the spectacle of a darkened theatre in which no one watches and no one plays.

OCTOBER

1st October

The Churches tried hard to strengthen their influence by making long overdue reforms but they did not set out to study the situation with which they were faced as an urgent immediate matter. They addressed the world on behalf of God in terms which grew less and less meaningful to the people they hoped to reach. They could offer less and less evidence of corporate living to question and challenge the life of the society in which they were set. They tended to foster a religion of pious, respectable and unadventurous enclaves. There were brilliant minds and devoted lives at the service of the Churches but the process of the eclipse of God went on because the more obviously influential factors at work in social life, whether cultural, economic, political or intellectual, pursued ends quite other than those of ecclesiastics.

The Churches paid dearly for having for so long committed the direction of their witness to clergymen whose education had been increasingly out of touch with the emerging world.

2nd October

Eclipse was a fitting symbol of what took place. It was a slow inexorable process, part wilfully determined, part unwittingly allowed to happen, in which the reality of relationship with God had been obscured and in which the ways of serving Him were blurred into general unspecific terms. To ancient faults new dangerous factors were swiftly being added. We must count in the legacy of superstition, of cursings, spells and witchcraft, of hideous exploitation of the fears of ignorant minds. We must include in it the scarcely-challenged cruelty of men to women and children, the shadow cast upon the very springs of human love. We must add in the persecution of heretics and the barbarities of religious wars. These

things breed other evils of suspicion and intolerance that infect
the body of believers, growing to fever-heat under conditions of
stress. The Church failed to deal wisely with the Enlightenment,
itself resisting new ways of thinking about human life on the earth
and giving grounds to its opponents to describe it as the enemy of
human progress.

3rd October

The nineteenth century was to see the rise to power of artists and
writers and secular teachers whose work at best evoked imagination and at worst played with the sentimentality and crude fantasy that a largely disinherited populace required. It was soon to put
to both crude and clever use the increasing knowledge of human
psychology which research in that field was to produce. In the
absence of acceptable religious symbolism still coarser substitutes
would be used. The more primitive appetites of humankind
became the object of quasi-religious practice ... The messianism
of Hitler met a need felt by millions of men and women. In him
they felt they encountered not simply the political saviour of a
society threatened with collapse, nor even a prophet of a new
social order, so much as an incarnation, a personal embodiment
of their own deepest selves and needs. They sought in him the
assurance of their own identity as persons, and a tangible bond
uniting the German race.

4th October

... White people who have entered Africa to reduce its peoples
and resources to serve only their own will found tides of rejection
rising to challenge them in the most vulnerable areas of their
psychological and spiritual life. White consciousness damaged
already by age-old rejection of Jews could not but feel still more
insecure in the face of coloured people's claims.

5th October

The Bible spares nothing to those who call God good. It records
crimes, tyrannies, disasters, cruelties falling upon all people. It

dares say that God creates Good and Evil, Darkness and Light. It says He both hides and reveals Himself, that He speaks and is also silent. The dumbness of God is a source of devout complaint. The biblical writers saw no reason to make light of the fury of God. They bowed to it in the full knowledge that His ways were not those of humanity. Even so they held fast to their trust in Him. "Though He slay me yet will I trust." Modern Judaism has not gone back upon that. In a Conservative Jewish prayer-book published in the United States the places of horror – the concentration camps – are deliberately named in the affirmation of faith. If indeed Jesus of Nazareth dying in agony upon the cross recited Psalm 22, it was wholly in keeping with Israel's maturest faith. "Every religion," wrote Pascal, "which does not affirm that God is hidden is not true," and in affirming that faith he himself committed himself to the God of Abraham, Isaac and Jacob.

6th October

Nevertheless the darkness and silence appal. The darkness and light are alike to Him, in the realm of darkness his wonders are known, but human beings are not God and but for His help we could not endure it. Those Jews and non-Jews who in the dark years took their lives were no cowards but men and women whom the darkness destroyed. It was not the unthinking or shallow who measured the horror but those who in fineness of spirit were overwhelmed.

This night sky of the Lord that has become the condition of our time and has been experienced in the anguish of the death camps and the bewilderment of multitudes of sufferers round the world is still, so faith affirms, the darkness where God is.

7th October

Bonhoeffer wrote, "Surely there has never been a generation in the course of history with so little ground under its feet as our own." He was speaking of the relation of human beings to reality, religion's business, and he went on to describe the time as one of no religion at all. He went on further to ask, as one who would not turn back in the darkness, how Christ could become the Lord of such displaced and disinherited men and women. Where and how could light be sought for such people?

8th October

Bonhoeffer's writings were made in conditions which signified how far the Christian churches had failed to embrace the Jewish conviction, how far as a consequence of such failure they had lacked the will to oppose the Caesarism of worldly powers and the ability to create wholly different patterns of living. In the darkness which he experienced to the full, having learned to see it as an ordeal of a whole people as well as a person, he grew more convinced of the nature of Christian intention. The true test of Christian faith lay in the 'worldliness' it called for and the participation in suffering that it entailed. Only so could men and women be caught up in the way of Christ, in the messianic event. Faith in Christ must commit them to the work of transforming the world through the relationships they themselves were ready to make. In all that men and women spoke or did to "the least of these my brethren" they received or rejected the Christ. Every act, every thought, every word, had thus become crucial. "The day will come," he wrote, "when men and women will be called again to utter the word of God with such power as will change and renew the world. It will be a new language which will horrify people, and yet overwhelm them by its power. It will be the language of a new righteousness and truth, a language which proclaims the peace of God with humanity and the achievement of His Kingdom."

9th October

The darkness may deepen in years ahead. There is as yet little to show that humankind in a wholly new spirit is seeking to build a quite different world, that the churches and faiths of humankind are possessed of a vision and will of a different kind from that which they manifested in the Holocaust years. Christianity's days of the eclipse of God may only now be beginning to be truly known. Times of great deprivation and of the purging away of futile and corrupted things may well lie ahead. It may very well be that the elder brother who has gone through such bitter times often before, the despised and rejected brother, may be needed the more to hold out a scarred yet sustaining hand.

10th October

We cannot fail to let the truth of the Holocaust be obscured or forgotten. It must be permitted to purge out the dross and the sin of the Church's life. It must compel them to hear all over again the question so often asked by the Jews: "Why do they hate us so?", and in turn ask their own question "Why the Jews?" Only so will the mystery of Israel's presence in the world be accorded its rightful place. Without it we lose our way. Perhaps we must learn to see the whole epoch of Christendom until now as something of a false start. Mighty works were done by it in His Name, but the ash of the Holocaust fires lies too deeply upon them today. Buber spoke of our time as a time of darkness but he also rejoiced to call it a night of expectation. It will only be so far as Christians are humbled enough to realize and admit that it was precisely in their wrongdoing to the people of Israel that they helped to darken the skies and went far to surrender God's world to the terror of the Abyss. They did so because they believed a lie and because they made it their business to maintain it, rejecting the people whom God had called.

11th October

The new beginning will only be made when those who committed this hideous wrong and those who were wronged learn to speak to each other in love. It is a formidable task, to take part in the redemption of a world that put into effect Operation Night and Fog, a world that had chosen for many centuries of its history to harbour the evil springs of that act. It is a task which will be undertaken only if men and women read the lesson of Golgotha–Auschwitz aright. Both Christian and Jew are therefore involved in presenting that lesson in all its truth to tomorrow's world. Those who ask God to deliver them must want to be free, to be freed from their own misdoing, their blindness and pride in the past.

They can only do that in truth when they seek out those whom they wronged and seek reconciliation with them. How much do Christians want to be free?

12th October

... in a last talk given by Rabbi Nachum Yanchiker to Jewish students on the eve of the German invasion of Lithuania, he counselled them not simply to try to stay alive but to "pour forth your words and cast them into letters ... For words have wings: they mount up to the heavenly heights and they endure for eternity." But time is needed for the words of poetry to be found, to be refined by fire and washed clean by water that they may so endure. From the camps and cellars there have come to us haunting lines like the now often quoted Cologne fragment:

> I believe in the sun even when it is not shining.
> I believe in love even when feeling it not.
> I believe in God even when He is silent.

There are other words too of still profounder insight, still surer grasp of what was being enacted. The time must come when words can be written and spoken that can inform human flesh anew and cause the hearts of men and women to burn with new hope and love, with the faith that God goes with them as they journey together.

13th October

The authors of the gospels all shared in the great Jewish religious tradition that bonded together God and His people, a tradition long since committed to writing in the scriptures but maintained as a living force by continuous dialogue within the community. Its basic attitudes best represented in the Psalms are those of trust and expectation. The opening verse of Psalm 40, "I waited patiently for the Lord: and he inclined unto me and heard my calling," sums up centuries of a relationship with God at once personal and corporate. Its note is to be heard in the Fourth Gospel in Jesus' words: "I knew that thou hearest me always" (11:42). That trust and expectation in its purity makes for the kind

of dependence which allows perfect freedom for development.
The forward movements of genuine spiritual growth are checked
when the trust begins to falter.

14th October

John stands among the great artists of the world as one not only
fortunate and blessed in the experience he had, not only eagle-
eyed in his powers of discerning truths, but as a master-craftsman
who found words and forms to express and share that vision with
others. He was both seer and builder. He saw emerging from the
words and works of Jesus the lineaments of a new life for human
beings. He sensed it in something whose creative stature was
comparable with primal creation. He sought not only to give formal expression to it to guide and sustain his fellow-disciples but
to prevent the vision itself being reduced in any way to conform
to popular expectations.

15th October

Few hearers of the passages read to them in church services, save
students and scholars, are concerned to identify the evangelist
who wrote them. If questioned they may well reply. "Does it matter?" Some will certainly answer that because it is God's word the
particular human instrument conveying it to us is not important.

Though I may not convince the latter I shall say that I believe
it matters greatly. The singularity of creatures in nature and in
human beings in particular is important. We hallow God's name
by observing this fact about them. It represents the growing tip of
the life that is His and in which we share. It is rightly observed,
however briefly, by bestowing a name on each child. The proof
that it matters comes uppermost when we learn to love someone,
loving them for being that person and no other.

16th October

It is no accident that John's is the gospel that turns wholly upon
the experience of loving ... I would claim it to be the most personal of all the gospels in the sense that is expressed in that phrase

concerning 'that disciple whom Jesus loved.' I do not suppose that
he did not believe that the love of Jesus did not extend to others.
He was ready to emphasise the point that "Jesus loved Martha,
and her sister, and Lazarus." (11:5) But he did face and take fully
the overwhelming fact that he was loved. His poem could well
carry the title that D. H. Lawrence would use, "Song of a man that
is loved". No one, I venture to think, would say that this does not
matter. It does not make the loved one a perfect artist or husband
or friend but it does make the best of that person with all his or
her gifts and failings ... John was no mean theologian but his
gospel is not a theological treatise. It is much more a sustained
reflection upon the realization that he was among those whom
Jesus loved.

17th October

John was convinced that the Spirit-powered church could deal
with its problems and hold together no matter what storms internal or external it had to endure. Without fear it could face whatever contemporary circumstances brought to bear upon it.

To do so it would have to be freed from the worldly assumptions about power, authority, glory and dignity which threatened
to infect and corrupt human relationships. John came to see that
in Jesus these things were not simply magnified to greater dimensions but as often as not completely reversed. It was a difficult lesson to learn and still is. A power that appeared powerless or a
glory that looked menial was hard to understand.

18th October

The story of the transfiguration is a deeply moving thing but
John's feet-washing story turns its notion of glory upside down.
John remembered the cry of Peter attempting to stay Jesus from
washing his feet as the voice of a man who finds himself being
swept from the customary moorings of his life, who knows that he
must yield or go away. He noticed that with characteristic aban-
don Peter yielded and stayed, but one other disciple perhaps at
that moment made up his mind that he must go. "As soon as Judas
had taken the piece of bread he went out." (13:30).

19th October

The image of birth was of course frequently used in the Jewish scriptures. It is an event of almost universal religious provenance. It is used freely in the description of religious experience today, and often much too glibly. At one point in the Johannine record of Jesus' teaching (16:21) it is chosen to give reassurance to the disciples facing their future work. More important still it is introduced early in the gospel (3:1-21) in the conversation with Nicodemus, and is one of the passages most in need of being reflected upon Psalter-wise. Birth is often difficult and dangerous, rebirth not likely to be easier, however we understand it. No timetable can be arranged for the labour pains of a group of people engaged in the process. For the hours of childbirth we must read years in the case of a new community. The suffering that this entails, the fears of those involved in it, the longing for peace and assurance that all is well, all have their full part ... In modern terms this gospel is a manual of obstetrics and post-natal care for the Christian communities. It is the wisest one ever written.

20th October

The members of the first Christian communities were Jews who had no idea of breaking away from the life of Israel to found a new religion, though their adherence to Jesus gave them a new sense of calling and direction and a new character. At some points they were distinctively committed to a way of life that distinguished them from Essenes, Zealots or Pharisees of certain traditions. They were drawn and held together by Jesus, spellbound though often baffled by his words. There is both pathos and realism in the phrase attributed to Thomas: "Lord, we do not know where you are going, so how can we know the way?" (14:5). In later years it was bound to become "We don't know where we are going either, but we trust you through the Holy Spirit to show us the way." This is the raison d'être of the Fourth Gospel.

21st October

What Jesus of Nazareth did, and what I believe John grasped more firmly than most people of that time, was to draw a few men and women round himself to begin living the life of the kingdom whose day had come. The unexpected so far transcended the expectations that the incredulity and hostility that is evident in John's narrative is itself a testimony to the leap of faith that it called for. Nor did it stop there. What John further envisaged and wrote into his gospel was the conviction that the job of the Christian communities lay not so much in preaching about Jesus but in furthering the new way of living sustained by the Spirit that he had bestowed on them.

22nd October

... learning to pray this gospel means becoming familiar with it as the language of the heart as generations of people have done with the Psalms, but using it as the poet suggests as scaffolding to help build the house of the Spirit in our world today. That means that we face the contemporary world scene in terms of religion ... Ours is not a time of no religion at all but one which raises acutely the question of what we mean by it.

23rd October

Our time has witnessed in fact a marked decline in membership of the major longstanding religious denominations accompanied by the growth outside them of a keener, more widespread interest in the nature of spirituality and its place in the total life of humankind. It has shown an impatience with theological propositions and ecclesiastical forms, but a much greater interest in personal relationships and the transcendent aspects of personal life. It may perhaps be described as a return to the concept of virtue as being, in Iris Murdoch's words, "the same in the artist as in the good man in that it is a selfless attention to nature: something which is easy to name but very hard to achieve." She goes on to say that a proper criterion of virtue is right action with the steady extension of the area of strict obligation. At first sight this would seem to many to offer no common ground because it left out God altogether. Not so, she replies, by suggesting that God could be the name of "a single perfect transcendent non-representable and necessarily real object of attention." That attention in religious terms is prayer which is the most heartfelt and fullest expression of love. It is no bad exercise to refrain from talking about God in order to give more attention in silence to the obligations of loving, a truly Johannine insight.

24th October

What had happened in history was nothing less than a loss of that immediacy of God in Christ which was the very core of the Johannine gospel. What was needed now was the discovery of God in human beings, in other words not by looking backwards to the historical Christ or to an imaginative figure compounded by devotional fervour, but to the men and women in whom through the Spirit he has chosen to live.

25th October

Being Jews they did not need convincing about God. What they needed was God not in the wonderful works he had done in the past but God in their midst. That need was being met. It could not have been more straightforwardly stated than by the simple words of Jesus of Nazareth, "To have seen me is to have seen the Father." (16:9) All else was illustration and suggestion of what this statement could mean. It is unlikely that John came any more quickly to understanding what it meant than other men and women who heard words to that effect, but his gospel may well have been what a work of art is to any artist who wrestles to bring it about, the way in which he discovers its meaning.

26th October

A religious attitude is that which is careful to pay full attention to people and things in the process of learning to love them. The contrary irreligious one is that which neglects to do this. It was never more tragically expressed than in Lear's anguished words: "Oh, I have ta'en too little care of this."

27th October

John had grasped the point that with the coming of the Logos–Christ into human history nothing could remain unaffected. John set out to show in the series of signs what had now to be faced.

There is something almost breathless in the unfolding of this. Religion freed from huckstering; sexual relations must find a way of giving women their rightful place, paternalism must be set aside, sectarian and tribalist divisions must cease, agonizing about the temple must give way to recognition of a profounder spirituality, the dispossessed of society must not be thrust back into making futile rebellions, the needy must be treated as of right, and mortality must not be allowed to be the great fearful negation of life. In very truth a greater than Moses is here, yet the situation is one that Moses himself foretold. Human history was not intended to culminate in the Exodus and the covenant. These were but Act One. Now Act Two had begun and the spiritually awake must take up their parts.

28th October

John details the steps by which the theme of the renunciation of power implicit in the very presence of Jesus in the world is upheld to the end. John had at a much earlier stage of his writing insisted that Jesus had accepted the taking of his life by the worldly powers as an unquestionable part of the task he had taken on, indeed was sent to do … he did not surrender his life that his friends might escape but that they might learn to live in his spirit and not that of the world.

29th October

John's passion story is hewn from the hardest imaginable rock. It is meant to bear the heaviest of burdens, a faithful contention with death. It brings into view the institutions of human polity, religious, military and judicial. In the midst of them it sets a prisoner. It confronts every reader with the common but terrible situation in which men can do to another man what they will. It is the moment when the Satan of this world lifts his head and laughs, when the victims must wonder if a different world could exist, or whether the idea that the world that we have can be loved is not dreadful mockery after all. Notice that but for the description of 'that disciple whom Jesus loved' repeated once more, there is no further reference to love in this gospel except in the added twenty-first chapter.

30th October

John wrote with the conviction that Jesus had completed the work he had been sent to do and that his last word from the cross meant simply that. Very briefly indeed he wrote into his account certain resurrection appearances, hinted at Ascension and concluded with a final reference to the gift of the Holy Spirit. Our journey round the outside looks somehow inconclusive if we expected something more incontrovertibly proven by all that had taken place. The end, it appears, is simply a beginning ... He stands before the world in the persons of those who believe in him, even though they have not seen anything more than someone dying with an unswerving trust in God.

31st October

Such an artist as John the poet proceeds by way of re-presentation. He recalls certain things in a way that permits us to enter into them now. To do so he makes use of words, imagery, references, feelings, and ideas which are already common to the life of his readers. In the gospels that means all the wealth of imagery that had been in constant use through Israel's history. It included those directly religious which spoke of God as Father, Judge, Maker and Ruler. It took from nature those of water and wind, fire and storms, bread and wine, light and darkness, birth and death. From Israel's history it drew imagery in such terms as Messiah, Son of God and Son of Man, the Spirit as dove, the temple as God's dwelling place among his people, the Passover and the covenant as the symbols of his relationship with them. Such imagery put to use century after century provided the forms through which this people discerned and responded to the reality of their very existence. We could liken it in visual terms to an enormous tapestry woven from the total experience of generations of men and women but to do so would run the risk of using too static an image. Hebrew symbolism is always expressive of action, of things being done and relationships entered into. For that reason too it swings between singing and keeping silent.

NOVEMBER

1st November

To learn how to read [the Fourth Gospel] aright means three things. First learning what the initial situation in which Jesus figured was like. In the second place understanding what the evangelist saw Jesus doing in it. Thirdly we have to translate what John wrote into terms which are relevant and meaningful today. All such reading of poetry is in a very real sense an act of personal translation. The miracle performed by words is nowhere more vividly shown than in the fact that through an immensely long chain of translations the poem John wrote reaches us today to draw us into the experience it expresses.

2nd November

The Christian communities must ... set out on a long march not in geographical terms with a charismatic leader like Moses, but no less deliberately breaking free from the power-structured society, religious and political, communal and personal, in which they had grown accustomed to live. It was in no sense to be an escape from history but a sober attempt to go through the birth pangs and travail of a new kind of community being born. It would involve persecution and most probably death even though it would try to live peaceably with everybody. It would neither turn its back on the world nor use worldly methods to overthrow its opponents. The test of its integrity would lie in its practice.

3rd November

The real test lay in whether they would try to think out and put into practice the new modes of living which their journey to freedom presupposed. How much self-criticism and internal dispute would they allow and encourage for the sake of the truth in living that they sought? Could they work with a sense of unity not imposed from above but inspired from all those participating in it? As we read the Fourth Gospel do we get from it deep conviction that the guidance of the Holy Spirit is a matter for real rejoicing?

4th November

Religion seen in terms of the Exodus is not a matter of things handed down but of confrontation, of coming up to a place where divine revelation and human discovery meet. As thought is born of failure, poetry derives its vital force from the poet's imaginative grasp and expression of what has hitherto eluded him. At that moment of 'kindling', as the Wordsworths called it, he is able to tell of something that alters his whole vision of life. Revelation is never a one-sided affair like filling a vessel. It is always participating in something between two parties.

5th November

Two classic illustrative moments of revelation which stand almost equidistant in time on either side of the Fourth Gospel may illustrate this. The first is that of Moses' experience at the burning bush. The theophany does not begin until he turns aside to look at it nor is it ever completed until his life ended. The second is begun at the moment when Dante, not quite nine years old, saw Beatrice Portinari at a May Day party, a girl younger than himself, and began to know that a god stronger than himself had touched him, kindled in him inspiration that would bear its fruit many years later in the greatest poem of medieval Europe. John tells us nothing of any such moment that began his discipleship though he may have been one of the two mentioned in the first chapter who stayed with Jesus. If then he be 'that disciple whom Jesus loved' spoken of later, the Fourth Gospel is a love story like the *Divina Commedia* itself.

6th November

John does not suggest that Jesus always entrusted himself to other people. He mentions a number of occasions when he actually withdrew from them because he judged that the right time for putting himself into their hands had not come. When it did come he held nothing back. It is part of the process of learning to love in parenthood, courtship, marriage, friendship and all social relations whatever, to know when and how to further the extending of trust.

7th November

A poem is more than words in the sense that a meal is more than the food on the table. In both cases it is the total behaviour of the people involved that is important. It is no accident that at the heart of the life and worship of the Christian community there is a meal in and through which the behaviour, the relationships, thoughts and purposes of it are cleansed, nourished and redirected. By constant return to the table of its original institution it draws new strength, clearer sense of purpose and enlarged understanding. As in good household meals it balances silence and glad table-talk. Both have their place in furthering the life of the community, large or small.

8th November

The distinctive Johannine note is sounded with Jesus calling his disciples 'friends' ... At this most profound and revealing point of his gospel John has turned to the expression of what is fundamental to the Exodus story. Summoned, aided, guided, inspired by God, man is seeking to fill the Deuteronomic text, "to love the Lord your God, to walk in all his ways." His spiritual education lies in learning to embody in human life the ways of "God, merciful, gracious, long-suffering, abundant in loving – kindness and faithfulness." The word that is used to sum up the fruit of that education is friendship.

9th November

Understanding of the Johannine meaning of friendship has not been made easier by the emphasis put upon sexual love in terms of romantic passion with an ever-increasing vehemence in the modern world ... The opportunity to advance to a fuller human life presented by the greatly extended expectation of the life span of both men and women, and the great gains made in knowledge of the nature of sexuality, must be seen to be one of the most important spiritual disclosures of our time.

At such a time men and women are summoned to go forward beyond the relations sufficient for simply meeting the needs of everyday life – a state still very far from being realized by vast numbers throughout the world – to those which allow for more gracious and ampler relations. Understanding what Jesus Christ meant by friendship may well be the task that has now to be faced with passionate commitment by men and women and nations alike.

10th November

Ernst Bloch once described the beginnings of the great religions of the world as 'impact craters'. They were the outcome and evidence of some powerful spiritual event, theophany, or revelation that had at some time struck human society as a meteorite or asteroid might strike this planet. They changed the religious life of a people. They introduced new concepts by means of which men and women tried to understand, describe and order their life. It was because in such cases they were felt to make a great break with ways of thought and behaviour that had so far prevailed that they could be compared with a sudden almost cataclysmic event. For good and ill they changed the course of human history and the character of human lives. It is not surprising that those who pioneered such changes were often regarded by others as subversive and dangerous people. Exile, imprisonment, persecution and even death have been the experiences they have incurred. On their disciples and immediate followers some similar hardships fell until such times as the new teaching had won acceptance.

11th November

The Gospel of John was and is, as already emphasised, an interpretation designed to confirm the faith of certain groups of his followers. It was to do so by rehearsing Jesus's teaching and behaviour in respect of a way of life to be followed. It offered clues as to the ways in which the problems concerning this way should be faced and resolved. It underpinned the praying which such groups would engage in to maintain their relationship with him and with God.

12th November

John was living in a world where authority meant something absolute, where the population was divided between free men and slaves ... The evil of slavery in the Graeco-Roman world lay not simply in the fact that vast numbers of human beings were treated with the most brutal inhumanity but that other men justified to themselves that inhuman relationship. To do so the Greeks, so proud of free citizenship in the city-state, argued that the slave was an inferior species of being. In Israel, though legally landless labourers and servants might not be enslaved but were 'hirelings' for six years, actual slavery did exist and masters could treat them as inferior beings. Along with such Hebrew hirelings went numbers of 'Canaanitish slaves' who were treated like cattle and shamefully abused. Their existence was evidence of the sick society which Israel had become and in which authority was finally represented by the infamous Herodian kings or the callous brutality of Roman officials. One may understand why the evangelist John never mentioned a Herod and treated the very word king with the utmost reserve.

13th November

The Gospels were being drawn in defiance of society's seemingly absolute power over people's lives towards a new way of life by one who had promised them that he had overcome that world's power. He had spoken of that life as of another realm, eternal life or the kingdom of God. No one they had ever known had spoken like this. No one else had shown to them such signs of a different ordering of human affairs. No one had lived it that way. Those who had followed and kept to him knew that somehow the choice had been his not theirs. Trusting him meant simply that. Who

would believe that as years slipped by? How could he be kept fresh
in their minds as one still amongst them? Looking back was not
what they wanted. Looking into what stayed with them and grew
ever more real to them was what all were in need of ... It was then
a great bid to get the picture right that led to this gospel being
written.

14th November

John was reserved about institutions. He knew that even among
twelve men there could be discussion as to who was the greatest.
He knew that some men yearned for authority and others welcomed it for not very good reasons. Becoming a larger community
meant that buildings and regulations, organizations and job-
direction would be needed ... What John was chiefly concerned
with was the still greater need to keep alive the original relationship which they had had in the presence of Jesus, the relationships
which that man had brought into being. In them lay the soul of
the movement. What would it profit the church if it gained the
whole world and lost that? In the figure of Jesus the servant they
had been shown the true image of human/divine personal life. In
years to come if they turned away from it and accepted some
other figures as more desirable for worldly life, would they not
need to recall his words: "Why do you go about to kill me?"

15th November

What the gospel says to all men and women who make up the
world is: "Love one another as I have loved you" or, put in another
way, "Go about your life as those who are loved." ... The new
society ... embodies this act of loving by establishing a community
of persons. The word for them will be long in coming because it
would need long experience and much failure to bring home to
those involved what was really at stake. It proved easier for
Christians to think and speak lengthily of the Persons of the
Godhead than to envisage human society in terms of persons. It
was in some sense a measure of the extent to which 'the man' of
the Fourth Gospel was obscured by the hierarchical imagery so
dear to the Roman political mind. What were lost to sight in the

processes of ecclesiastical organization were the radical relationships that obtained where two or three were gathered together. As
the numbers of adherents to the Christian communities grew, was
it possible to retain the spirit and character of the personal
relations they had once known?

16th November

What did 'the man' do? The symbols employed in the story of the
feeding of the multitude are clear. There are limited resources but
responsibility must be accepted and common action taken. Waste
is to be avoided. An attempt to hasten the end by making this man
king had to be avoided ... The Kingdom of God for whose coming the Christian communities waited and worked must have its
own times of growth. Those who hungered for it must in patience
possess their souls, make mistakes but learn from them in penitence and trust, and above all remain attentive to the Spirit. They
must not lose sight of the pattern of true human relationships
which they had been introduced to by this man. Tested day after
day by every conceivable problem they must learn how it could be
extended to become universal.

17th November

Jesus looked men and women, Jews and Samaritans, Greeks and
Romans, learned and ignorant, friendly and hostile, in the eye to
make contact with them as human beings, as potential friends. He
drew a few of them to himself to embody that way of living so
that it might under God be the way forward for humankind. It
required of them a great act of believing in him because for the
moment there was little to show for it but tribulation and pain and
death. The evangelist John understood what it meant, not any
better perhaps than some few named and many more nameless
men and women did, but in a way that he could put into words.
He did that because he was a poet and that is a poet's job.

18th November

In the letter of the Churches of Vienne and Lyons, describing the cruel martyrdoms suffered by many Christians in AD 177, there is a notable sentence. It says that those who witnessed them "saw during the contest, even with the eyes of flesh, in the person of their sister, Him who was crucified for them, to assure those who believed on Him that everyone who suffereth for the glory of Christ hath for ever fellowship with the living God." The brief testimony to St. Blandina deserves to be better known. It says very plainly and simply that those witnesses to that terrible event saw Jesus Christ in a woman. She is sharing for ever a fellowship in the divine.

19th November

… bear in mind that as late as 1889 English judges ruled that the word person in English statutes did not include women. Practice made clear what this could mean in social life. For all but a few it meant suffering inflicted upon women quite simply because they were legally and socially weaker than men. To be so disadvantaged in a world where the power game is judged to be all-important is to be at the mercy of those who will win. The allotting of spoils – "to every man a damsel or two" – may have changed some of its forms, but the overall outcome has remained much the same both in Christian and other societies until very recent times. To be born of a woman is a plain fact, to be born a woman has been for the most part a misfortune.

20th November

It is clear from the New Testament that women played an important part in shaping the new communities of Christians, as St. Paul willingly admitted. He was greatly indebted to them and at one point ready to dismiss the sexual distinction. From that position he later retreated and in his most authoritative manner insisted on their subordination to men. He insisted that they should be silent because theirs was a secondary role and woman herself the primal transgressor. At no far distant time such sexual repudiation would harden into an ecclesiastical system and fill the world with a tradition of sexual guilt.

21st November

It is difficult to escape the conclusion that the two evil legacies of the failure of Christendom to treat women as persons of equal dignity with that of men, which resulted on the one hand in the hatred and contempt from the times of the Fathers until that of Schopenhauer and Strindberg, and on the other in the false romanticism from the Troubadours to Ruskin and the Pre-Raphaelites, were equally poisonous. Neither of them is quite dead today both within and outside the churches.

22nd November

To deprecate or lose sight of the feminine is to weaken the sense of the relatedness which must lie at the heart of a religious sense of reality, the truth of which is set out in the Johannine account of what Jesus said at the last supper with his disciples. The imagery used by Jesus throughout his teaching whether in materials like bread, wine and water or in the actions of shepherding, serving and feeding is that which highlights relationships and dependency … It is for this reason that the Fourth Gospel sums up the truth of such relatedness in terms of loving. It omits the familiar imagery of the ruler and servants, the judge and the punished, the despot and the obedience he exacts, all of which belonged to the male conception of governance and power, and all of which beget fears of being questioned, and displace trust by an anxiety to please. What is really at issue in this is not so much whether the name and pronouns used for God are masculine, but whether the active relationship between God and his people is that which primarily expressed the truth that God's only power is that of loving. To learn what that means both sexes have to learn afresh what the feminine in human life expresses.

23rd November

What the wedding at Cana story was meant to make clear was that marriage could be the channel of opportunity for both sexes to learn what loving meant. The truth about what was actually happening is blurted out by the older woman because she has seen it all happen before. The male-dominated society has too limited a view of what is needed. It has not tried to learn from woman's love what it discloses of God's relationship to human beings ... John's story is a sad realistic assessment of what has been done to marriage hitherto, depriving it of that abundance of good wine that it could provide for successive stages of life. It is not the only field of education in which humanity has acted in cruelly mechanical ways, and failed as yet to enable men and women to learn the truth about themselves and others, but it is for most of us the most important, which is why John gave it its place of priority.

24th November

In the male-dominated world the Samaritan woman is indomitable. She has learned how to hold her own. Symbolically she is the drawer of water, ... the ocean from which life and love have sprung. In herself as a person she is quick-witted, resourceful, defensive, and if need be deceitful. She has established a relationship with men which is not simply 'and'; it has with some practice become that of 'but.' No other conversation in the Fourth Gospel has the same give and take character as this. Pure invention on John's part it may be, but its significance is overwhelming. Here is the first truly apostolic figure called into being by Jesus, a Samaritan and a woman.

25th November

A human household for a moment is happily revealed – "Jesus loved Martha and her sister and Lazarus" – but the shadow of death has been cast upon it. Death as a fact in living is being taken into the story and John chose to do this through women. Men have no doubt attached to it either brutal matter-of-factness or a mystical dimension. It has fallen to women to take death into the daily task of living. It is right that they should be those through whom the first steps are taken to grasp death with loving trustful hands.

26th November

In this final sign-story before the putting to death of Jesus, John made symbol and parable go as far as they could. They tell us nothing of resurrection life save that love sustains whatever meaning it can have. They are not meant to forestall the death on the cross with an assurance that death could not take him away, but to turn the reader's attention to something which was shown in the life, death and resurrection of Jesus Christ, that is to say that the power of God is nothing else but the power of loving. Against the reality of the meaninglessness, futurelessness and powerlessness that such a possibility or probability as annihilation by nuclear warfare holds out to humankind, it maintains a trust in such loving.

27th November

Mary Magdala should hold her unique position quite clearly as the first witness to the risen Christ, the first bearer of apostolic commission, and being in person for some hours the confessing church on earth. Hers is the voice that speaks through the ages with tender concern and uninhibited joy for Jesus Christ's sake. In the course of the Fourth Gospel we come a long way from the unnamed and unnoticed bride of the first story to this Mary greeted by the risen Christ and it is unlikely that John wanted it otherwise ... It was a small thing no doubt that the commemoration of St Mary Magdalene which had its place in the first Prayer Book of Edward VI should have been removed from the second, but it showed how reformers were minded to think of women.

28th November

That appearances had a place in the early tradition of the Church is undeniable. Whether they were more than partly symbols of devotion and partly products of pious imagination is a matter of conjecture. The appearance of Jesus in the Apocryphal Gospels and many books of Acts are evidence of the bizarre lengths to which the latter could go. What John was concerned to do was to free belief in the presence of the Spirit, given to the Church by

Jesus, from dependence upon such things, no matter how reliable an authority could be quoted to support them. Resurrection was something to be experienced in the day to day living of the disciples. "We know that we have passed from death to life because we love the brethren." It was too real a matter of present relationships to need substantiation from appearances or even scriptural authority. It would contradict the whole burden of John's Gospel to direct the believer's attention backwards. The trust and the love with which he was most concerned needed no such authorization.

29th November

No other gospel gives such attention to personal relationships, to the truth that our relation to God is that which shows itself in our relation to fellow human beings. Resurrection comes late in the narrative but it comes as something prepared for step by step in the uncovering of the relationship Jesus had with his disciples. Much of it they very plainly did not understand until at and after his death ... Men and women were caught up into a new kind of life of which Jesus had told them and brought them into. It was realization of what Joel's prophecy had spoken: "I will pour out my Spirit upon all flesh, and your sons and daughters shall prophesy." The relationships of worldly powers would give place to those of agape and the daughters would take their place as of right in the new community of the Spirit.

30th November

In matters of sex the Christian Church retreated from the opportunity glimpsed in its earliest days of drawing out in actual living the implications of the belief that God had taken the flesh of humanity as his body, making it holy. What sadly becomes evident in Paul's treatment of women's part in the life of the Church is his inability to overcome a deep distrust of sexuality and a fear that women's freedom to express themselves uncontrolled by men must bring chaos into human relations. "It is a good thing for a man to have nothing to do with women." Whatever is connected with sex is dangerous and to be avoided. Safety – and Paul rarely envisages a more positive relationship than this – therefore lies in the domestic seclusion of women, strict control of their dress, and subordination to male authority. The sins of the flesh to which women are the temptresses are the most defiling. Other sins are 'outside the body', those of sex defile the Lord's temple which is the body. He went on to allow a prophylactic marriage without ever supposing that it was a final insult to women.

DECEMBER

1st December

... the human experience of Christians has refused to be bound by the theoretical distinction and gradually forced recognition of the need to bring eros and agape together. It is this which underlies the long struggle to bring men and women together as joint heirs of the grace of God and to give to their sexual relations a sacred dignity. Grace is not given to oust or subdue nature represented by eros but to bring it to perfection. For too many centuries Christians looked at life through the filters of doctrine that obscured and distorted their views of the body and their sexuality. They were largely unready to learn from each other the truth about themselves and nowhere more unwilling to do so than in the relations of men and women. Education as a life process, which is far wider and more profound than literacy can afford us, was but fitfully admitted. It could and did gather recognition by escaping from theological control and finding channels for itself in the arts and sciences.

2nd December

The place that John gave in his gospel to women was the basis upon which a new understanding of agape could be built. Without it sexual love would be for ever made a rival or an enemy to the divine love whereas what John was making way for was the very opposite of that. It would take eros into itself and begin the long process of learning how human beings through every cell of their bodies might learn to glorify God.

3rd December

John did not go on to describe how love might be between a man and a woman but his gospel shows no trace of fear with regard to sex, but a readiness throughout to trust that uncovering process which the Spirit would use to bring human beings to a glad recognition of their mutual self-giving in love. John did not think fit to bring agape into his prologue but reserved a place for it in that declaration of divine intent which he used in reply to the question of Nicodemus. God loved the world so much that he set light and life in it in the person of Jesus Christ that for love's sake the world might be saved. There is nothing here of judgment and condemnation, of punishment and sacrificial atonement but simply a total dependence upon love. He has taken human flesh, born of a woman, that the miracle might be wrought in that flesh.

4th December

I believe that John dreaded the creation of a new priesthood of men to exercise in the Christian communities one more variant form of priesthood that men had set up in the ancient world, as if foreseeing what Blake would one day lament as he looked at the garden of Love:

> And Priests in black gowns were walking their rounds,
> And binding with briars my joys and desires,

and for that reason gave to women in his gospel as full a measure of the shared ministry of both sexes as he could. It was doomed not to succeed but the seed planted by Jesus of Nazareth did not wither away.

5th December

Slowly and with many false starts the movement for the emancipation of women from the subjection to which for many centuries they had been condemned made headway as Héloïse and her successors found voices to cry out, and poets, novelists, and playwrights helped to create a more imaginative perception of womanhood. Without it the agape which is the vitalizing theme of the Fourth Gospel must remain simply a word deprived of the flesh and blood that enables it to become an active force in the world. Only a divinized love, an eros set free to become conjugal, and able to show men and women how to love instead of dreaming about it, could bring mankind and womankind to a true grasp of sexuality redeemed. John intimated that the revelation of its undying presence in the world would be brought to men by the woman.

6th December

If we have in our minds a notion of a Church that apparently is not there, it may well be that that was not the kind of thing John believed Jesus was concerned with. Our picture of the Church may be obscuring his. Time after time in this gospel John dwelt on the mistaken reactions of both friends and opponents to what Jesus did and said. It carries the warning that if it could happen then, when people were face to face with Jesus, how much more likely it will be that they can get things wrong almost a generation later. Opponents have grown more bitter in their hostility. Believers are tempted to assume that they know how things are or should be.

7th December

The new life and the new way in Jesus would be all too quickly lost to sight if Christians accepted without careful and prayerful concern relationships within the ecclesia that belonged to the very world they were being called upon to renounce. Convinced that Jesus had set before them a very different expression of apostolicity, John was determined to concentrate all attention on that. Whether he had read Paul's letters or not, he turned away from the authoritarian tone to a patient attempt to keep the picture of the servant Jesus before his readers. As I have stressed earlier the feet-washing scene must be treated as of cardinal importance ... At the very least a new look at all authority, parental, political, rabbinic, priestly, was called for because it was exploited to lay burdens upon human beings instead of fulfilling its true purpose of fostering growth.

8th December

... the end-term of the Johannine vision of what Jesus was about was the one-ness or unity for which he prayed. It means nothing less than integration of all human faculties, desires, and powers in a process of living which satisfies personal and social hungers. Men and women create religions, empires, arts and sciences to gain measures of integration. Two things beset them with dangers throughout; their lack of self-knowledge and their changing world. Their own partial achievements become obstacles to their continued growth. Turned into idols, religious or secular, they not only blind their adherents but make them turn fiercely upon whoever or whatever is felt to challenge their continuance. The impact crater, as we have called it earlier, is just such a moment in history when in one man's life a wholly new principle of integration confronts the society that is far gone in disintegration. Such was Jewish society when Jesus the Nazarene came forward and called men and women to a new way of life. On his head broke the fury of those who chose suicide rather than a new mode of living.

9th December

What John has seen and set out in dramatic fashion throughout his gospel is that the terrible radical imperfections of men and women, their blindness, their selfishness, their self-righteousness, their murderous hatred, cannot defeat this thing which is at work as the result of the coming of Jesus. That is what it means to affirm that the Church is holy, a channel of God's grace for the continuing of his work in the world.

10th December

In the power of the Spirit a new Israel must come into being, a community of peoples in whose relationships a new common life begins to take shape. The God and Father of all humankind sent his Son that the fratricidal wounds of the world's history might be healed, that all nations might come to a peaceful co-existence. The Church catholic of the Johannine vision is not one withdrawn from the world but a community in which reconciliation has become the truth incarnate in its manner of living. From the seed thus planted must grow that tree of life "whose leaves were for the healing of the nations."

11th December

… of all the canonical gospels that of John most clearly defines the universal objective of the community that comes into being through Jesus and is activated by the Holy Spirit. It exists to give effect in action to the truth that we are members one of another. One part of its task is to scrutinize the relationships which actually obtain in the societies like nation-states, churches, cities, industrial enterprises, educational institutions, and leisure activities, to assess their reality. Do they really express a belonging to one another or an idealized gloss on the situation which masks varying degrees of apartheid? Is the welfare of the weakest members of all those involved the primary concern of the strongest? In calling the one God the Father of all do we seek universal community as the active expression of our faith?

12th December

From scrutiny the Church must pass to action to repair what is faulty, to supply what is missing, to challenge what obstructs it. Its business like that of its Lord is to give itself as food for the life of God's people without exception … To say this with the history and present state of the Church catholic in mind is to be made painfully aware of the extent to which an idealized form of religion has been substituted for its practice. Belatedly it has begun to examine some aspects of the world it faces, the still hideous subjection of women, the remorseless exploitation of weak underdeveloped peoples, the squalor of the down-town lots of great cities, the blatant differentials of education, racial hatred, anti-Semitism. It has made some gestures of great value in all these fields, but with too little overall sense of purpose binding all local congregations together to serve as one body.

13th December

... that they may be so completely one ... is first and foremost a
unity of personal life which rejects dualist thought that divides
body and spirit, the spiritual from the material world, the earthly
from the heavenly, the theoretical from the practical. It is secondly
a unity of humanity that rejects whatever divides human society
and impedes the growth of genuine community on earth.

14th December

Having grasped the universal significance of the work of Jesus
and stated it clearly: "there is neither Jew nor Greek, neither
bond nor free, neither male nor female," Paul was overtaken
by the realities of estrangement in the world he lived in and
fell back upon counselling submission to the conventional social
relationships of the day, urging charity but otherwise bowing
to them. So for eighteen centuries many Christians would up-
hold slavery and even fight for its continuance, and for that
time too would persecute Jews and deny personal equality to
women.

15th December

As mortal and fallible human beings we must not treat human
works as absolutes. The New Testament, written indeed by men
inspired by the Holy Spirit, is neither historically nor theological-
ly an absolute set beyond human limitations, any more than our
subsequent interpretations of it can claim to be. There is none
good in the absolute sense but God.

16th December

John wanted to make room in his gospel for human imagination
to be free and fearless enough to transcend all those titles of
Messianism that men and women were accustomed to using. He
sought to awaken them to spiritual response such as no one as
yet had discerned. His own task as a poet was not just to make
the words that were familiar mean more than most people had

ever guessed, but to call on his fellow-Christians to make the imaginative leap that loving inspires.

17th December

To his own generation, to secure the fullest co-operative response, John appealed by making use of the great themes of Messiah and Logos, Son of God and Son of Man, interwoven dramatically with the events of the life, death and resurrection of Jesus. He did what every poet and artist must do to be read at all, while keeping open his own line along which he is free to say what is his uniquely personal thing. Where poets fail to hold these in balance they becomes either prisoners to current understanding and taste or largely unintelligible and therefore neglected.

18th December

The great bulk of the Fourth Gospel is taken up with a description of personal relations. It could be said to begin with Jesus inviting some men to stay with him and learn from that personal contact what manner of man he was. From then on they were given the opportunity to watch and listen to him as he faced the critics of what he was doing. It was evident that he crossed social barriers, that he was deeply concerned with the marginalized people of society, that he saw no reason why current styles of behaviour should not be challenged, and that while he was prudent he was also fearless. John realized quickly that this manner of living was what Jesus meant by loving.

19th December

Believing in God was not subscribing to what people said of him but responding to what God required of those he confronted. To become alive to a world understood in that way was to gain a wholly new vision of it. One had to decide to be for or against it on the basis of trusting Jesus.

20th December

Here is the man who had drawn them to himself, who had loved them and taught them the meaning of love. Here was the man crucified by the demonic evil powers of the world, but the man who had quite simply conquered it by giving his whole life for the sake of the world's lost children. Here was the man who had broken through all the barriers that divided men and women from each other and built up between them distrust and fear. Here was the man who had shown equal understanding of men and women, who had shown both grief and hope in the way through suffering and death, who had taught them the meaning of trust in the simplest channels of everyday life.

21st December

But something more had yet to be said of this man, the hardest and strangest thing that, but for all that had gone before and had taken place since, it would have been almost impossible to speak rightly. This man had died. Some of this friends had had moments thereafter when he appeared to be among them confirming his words that they would see him again, confirming the promise that he would give them the Holy Spirit. But, and here I think John is quietly adamant, this was not what the Johannine Christ must be thought to be, however moving the experience to those who claimed to have seen him. To a woman, Mary of Magdala, to a man, Thomas, one of the Twelve, the word is the same: "Don't cling to the vision to make a glory of thy silent pining." What matters is the trust in God that he begot in you, the trust through which you will have access to God for every moment of your life. Personal life is finite but every moment of it can become significant of eternal life and incandescent with glory. That was how the Johannine Christ had lived among them. That was what he had promised they would come to know 'through him' and by his being 'amongst them'. What he had been was closed in human terms as a thing of the past, what he was in human hearts and minds they were now and henceforth for ever committed to learn through the Holy Spirit who would be with them and in them. Because he the Johannine Christ had been, they were new men and women.

22nd December

Prophets still for most people are biblical characters or those with some insights into the future. They do not see them as men and women who search for the truth in every human situation and tell us what it looks like no matter how unpopular or demanding it is. They do not expect the Holy Spirit to be as disturbing as this. What enthusiasm for the Spirit there is tends to express itself in acts of personal piety and charitable concerns. All too rarely does it recognize the confrontation of ways of life in the world in which it becomes necessary to take sides.

23rd December

They were learning that God the Spirit was to be worshipped, in and through, not holy places nor traditional offerings but the life of the holy community and the relationships within and outside it … That new life expressed itself in loving. It was the presence of the Holy Spirit that made loving possible and actual. So John made his book culminate in one scene in which Jesus breathed into men and women the spirit or breath of this new life.

24th December

John did what no other evangelist did with the basic story. He treated the death, resurrection and ascension of Jesus as nearly as possible as one event. He made it the condition of the Spirit's coming, and that outpouring of Spirit the consummation of everything that had had its place in the story. Not a word here about giving his life a ransom for many or atonement, mediation, or sacrifice, but simply that this is the way by which the Holy Spirit has been given.

25th December

The fear that would hold human beings back from being unafraid of admitting errors and willing to seek correction can be overcome by loving, since loving is essentially an unobstructed acceptance of the other, whether material or personal, which enables what is potential to be realized. The call "Follow me" made by Jesus is a call to be 'what you are', a child of God who is wholly concerned to bring you and his whole creation to its wholeness of living.

26th December

They prefer to act as the children of the devil, 'a murderer from the beginning' and 'the father of lies'. Once again we are faced with the demand to honour the Spirit of truth. The devil means literally 'the slanderer'. We slander those whom we fail to love. By permitting the slander to become a habit or tradition we build walls of hatred.

27th December

They are not to be a self-confirming, self-justifying group whose unity is predetermined, but one that can receive and hold together the contraries that living introduces them to, long and patiently enough to be able to resolve the tensions set up by moving on to new stages of relationship with one another. Their unity must be in the first place the psychic unity which was adumbrated in the experience of the children of Israel, and which at some early stages in the history of other peoples was implanted in their members by acts of religious affirmation using symbols of death and rebirth.

28th December

The essential legacy of John ... remains, and its true manifestation is the outpouring of the Spirit of which the gospel-poem was one of its purest effusions and to which it was to recall hungry and eager souls from that time until now. The lives of the prophets, saints, artists, poets, as much as those of the most ordinary men and women, are not success stories viewed in this dimension. They are compact of many defeats, wasted efforts, frequent disappointments, and cruel failures, but their contribution has lain in the continuance of hope beyond all things and is flowering in new gestures of trust in the Christ–Spirit alive with us still. "They" as

Jesus said in the prayer ascribed to him, "are in the world" and "in them I am glorified."

29th December

John somewhat strangely chose to leave out many striking things that have belonged to the Christian story: no Lord's Prayer, no words recalling the Eucharistic meal, no sending out men to baptize or to preach, no transfiguration, no Pentecostal public scene, no attempt to described the Ascension. What he dwelt upon rather was that series of signs, the disturbances that they aroused, the conflict Jesus chose not to turn away from, but to go through with the promise to those who trusted in him that the thing they had shared would not fail.

30th December

We take from the Fourth Gospel finally the great conviction that the Spirit of God is at work in the world, in the hearts of men and women, in young and old, in simple as well as talented people, in the failures and those apparently successful, in all faiths and nations. We take furthermore the demand of the Spirit that we be ready staff in hand and with expectation to move forward into a world as yet unknown. This also entails times of patient waiting, of acceptance without losing hope, of manifest failures and grievous sins, of reconditioning to have a new sense of initiative for the journey ahead. It means finding the Spirit at work in all manner of channels of events and human labour. It means learning as Jesus of Nazareth did to listen, see, touch and taste all God-given things, that we may be the better equipped to respond to this prompting Spirit. It also means being warned that the Spirit blows where it listeth and, as Max Plowman wrote in *Bridge into the Future* (1944), "If you canalize the wind with a stone drain pipe it isn't wind that you get but a draught." It means finally that we go on our way rejoicing in the day that is still to come, the day when Jesus Christ's presence through the Spirit is known to God's people on earth.

31st December

1. Prayer is the effort that each of us makes to be as honest as possible about life, our own, that of others we know, and of the society in which we live. This is what the Psalmist meant by asking for a clean heart. Prayer that does not strive to be honest is pseudo-prayer and not worth the time spent on it.

2. Because it is very difficult to be honest to God the old Jewish counsel about preparing to pray is of the utmost importance here. Some teachers said that the preparation was as important if not more so than the praying. It might give us pause to think what such honesty really means and what it asks of us in respect of our own personal life, our relations with others and with God. This goes a good deal deeper than the customary acts of self-examination and for that reason is best taken slowly. It has to be worked away at, which is why a regular effort is important.

3. It is important to remember that we are not alone in setting about this. Three times in John's gospel Jesus speaks of "not being alone." It is not our business to try to imagine ourselves in the presence of God but as simply as possible to remind ourselves that it is so.

4. We are also members of the whole family of God. The gospel we are reading and trying to pray is about the life of that family, about its present condition and the hope of redemption. It is part of the business of being honest to remember this. In praying the gospel we are taking part in the history of the redemption of the world no less than those first disciples.

5. The Fourth Gospel is the great canticle of the Spirit at work in the world. It was written to sustain the hope of all those who look for the coming of God's kingdom on earth. We must learn to sing it, audibly or silently, by listening to it, by being anguished and delighted by it, as a documentary of the present-day world.

6. The Fourth Gospel did not promise the disciples a future free from tribulation, but one in which they would not be overcome. We are to read it as the lifeline that renews in us the sense of God coming into the world.

AND SO TO NEXT YEAR

And for the first three months of next year we might do well to follow
Alan Ecclestone's suggestion that we pray the Fourth Gospel as
poem. Here, with some minor changes, is his ninety-day plan of
reading:

1	1.1–5	21	6.41–51	41	9:35–41
2	1.6–8	22	6.52–59	42	10:1–10
3	1.9–13	23	6.60–71	43	10:11–18
4	1.14–18	24	5.1–18	44	10:19–28
5	1.19–28	25	5.19–29	45	10:29–42
6	1.29–42	26	5.30–38	46	11:1–16
7	1.43–51	27	5.39–47	47	11:17–27
8	2.1–12	28	7.1–13	48	11:28–44
9	2.13–22	29	7.14–24	49	11:45–57
10	2.23–25	30	7.25–31	50	12:1–8
11	3.1–15	31	7.32–39	51	12:9–19
12	3.16–21	32	7.40–52	52	12:20–24
13	3.22–36	33	7.53–8.11	53	12:25–28
14	4.1–14	34	8:12–20	54	12:29–36
15	4.15–26	35	8:21–30	55	12:37–43
16	4.27–42	36	8:31–38	56	12:44–46
17	4.43–54	37	8:39–47	57	12:47–50
18	6.1–15	38	8:48–59	58	13:1–20
19	6.16–24	39	9:1–17	59	13:21–30
20	6.25–40	40	9:18–34	60	13:31–38

61	14:1–14	71	16:29–33	81	19:23–30
62	14:15–21	72	17:1–11a	82	19:31–37
63	14:22–26	73	17:11b–19	83	19:38–42
64	14:27–31	74	17:20–23	84	20:1–10
65	15:1–8	75	17:24–26	85	20:11–18
66	15:9–17	76	18:1–14	86	20:19–23
67	15:18–27	77	18:15–27	87	20:24–31
68	16:1–11	78	18:28–40	88	21:1–14
69	16:12–24	79	19:1–13	89	21:15–19
70	16:25–28	80	19:14–22	90	21:20–25

SOURCES

THE SCAFFOLDING OF SPIRIT

The Scaffolding of Spirit

December

1	p. 78	11	p. 95	22	pp. 115–116
2	p. 79	12	pp. 95–96	23	pp. 116, 118
3	pp. 79–80	13	p. 96	24	p. 119
4	p. 81	14	p. 97	25	p. 122
5	p. 81	15	p.105	26	p. 123
6	p. 84	16	p. 106	27	p. 124
7	pp. 90–91	17	p. 108	28	p. 126
8	p. 93	18	pp. 110–111	29	pp. 126–127
9	pp. 93–94	19	p. 111	30	pp. 128–129
10	p. 95	20	pp. 112–113	31	pp. 131–132
		21	p. 113		